Traces & Trajectories

Traces & Trajectories:

The University of Texas at Austin School of Architecture at 100

edited by Richard L. Cleary

Traces and Trajectories:
The University of Texas at Austin School of Architecture at 100

Editor
Richard L. Cleary

Senior Assistant Editor and Researcher
Samuel Dodd

Assistant Editor and Researcher
Elise King

Production Editor
Christine Wong

Publication of *Traces and Trajectories* was made possible by the generous support of the Amon G. Carter Foundation

Photographs, illustrations, and selected texts by permission

Design: Cameron Kraus
Printed in the United States, the Whitley Printing Co.

ISBN 978-0-934951-14-2

Library of Congress Cataloging-in-Publication Data

Traces and trajectories : the University of Texas at Austin School of Architecture at 100 /
Richard L. Cleary, editor.
    p. cm.
    ISBN 978-0-934951-14-2
    I. University of Texas at Austin. School of Architecture--History. 2. Architecture--
    Study and teaching (Higher)--Texas--Austin--History. I. Cleary, Richard Louis.
    II. University of Texas at Austin. School of Architecture. III. Title: University of Texas
    at Austin School of Architecture at 100.

 NA2300.U57T73 2010
 720.71´176431--dc22
                                                                  2010036075

Table Of Contents

HUGO KUEHNE

FREDERICK E. GIESECKE

GOLDWIN GOLDSMITH

WALTER ROLFE

1909 BS in Architecture
1912 MS in Architecture
1912 Architecture library

1926 BArch

1933 Goldsmith Hall opens
1934 MArch

1910   1920   1930   1940

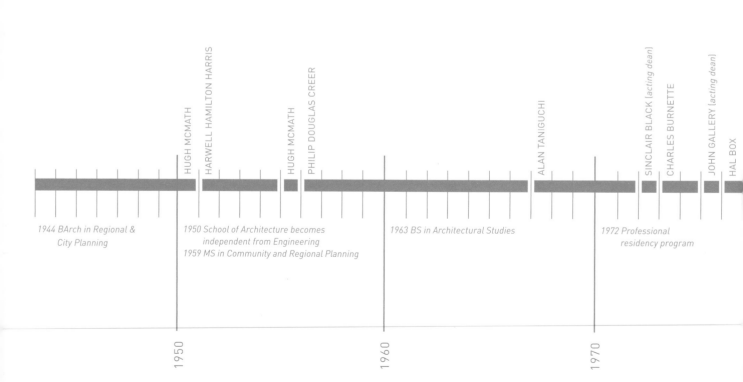

HUGH MCMATH

HARWELL HAMILTON HARRIS

HUGH MCMATH

PHILIP DOUGLAS CREER

ALAN TANIGUCHI

SINCLAIR BLACK (acting dean)

CHARLES BURNETTE

JOHN GALLERY (acting dean)

HAL BOX

*1944 BArch in Regional &
City Planning*

*1950 School of Architecture becomes
independent from Engineering*
1959 MS in Community and Regional Planning

1963 BS in Architectural Studies

*1972 Professional
residency program*

1950

1960

1970

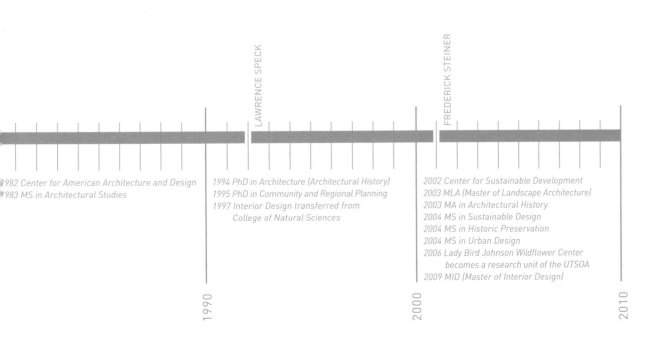

LAWRENCE SPECK

FREDERICK STEINER

1982 Center for American Architecture and Design
1983 MS in Architectural Studies

1994 PhD in Architecture (Architectural History)
1995 PhD in Community and Regional Planning
1997 Interior Design transferred from
       College of Natural Sciences

2002 Center for Sustainable Development
2003 MLA (Master of Landscape Architecture)
2003 MA in Architectural History
2004 MS in Sustainable Design
2004 MS in Historic Preservation
2004 MS in Urban Design
2006 Lady Bird Johnson Wildflower Center
       becomes a research unit of the UTSOA
2009 MID (Master of Interior Design)

1990   2000   2010

Foreword: Human Capital

Frederick Steiner, Dean, School of Architecture; Henry M. Rockwell Chair in Architecture. Dean since 2001.

The success and advancement of universities depend on people. As a human enterprise, we endeavor to attract the best and brightest students, to recruit and retain the most talented faculty, to maintain a highly skilled and motivated support staff, and to be relevant to our friends and alumni. This combination enables us to graduate individuals who change the world for the better.

Considerable resources and commitment are required to be successful in this human talent business. We are engaged in a highly competitive and expensive endeavor. Schools of architecture are particularly competitive and costly. The best universities in the world offer degrees in architecture, planning, landscape architecture, and interior design. Of these, the finest house cross-disciplinary, innovative programs in sustainability, architectural history, historic preservation, and urban design.

Because of our emphasis on studios and other forms of hands-on learning, schools of architecture and planning are especially expensive. To be most effective, studios have relatively small groups of students and are taught by professors with considerable theoretical depth and practical know-how. This includes numerous faculty members who are practicing architects, interior designers, landscape architecture, planners, and preservationists.

This combination of theory and practical knowledge is a hallmark of our School of Architecture. Many schools strive for this balance; very few achieve it. The pages that follow illustrate how we merge theory and practice, always valuing both and their interactions.

As Kurt Lewin observed, "there is nothing so practical as a good theory."[1] In essence, that is our job at a leading research university: the production of good theories, those that drive and redefine practice.

Comparitively, we certainly have a solid base in this regard. As dean, I stand on the shoulders of giants. My immediate predecessors, Larry Speck and Hal Box, guided our school for twenty-five years and did much to establish our high quality. In addition, they have been wonderful mentors to me. Hal, Larry, and I also inherited much from previous leaders of our school. Harwell Hamilton Harris recruited the best emerging minds in the world. Alan Taniguchi rejected the "bigger is better" ethos of the time, limiting enrollment, and increasing the quality and diversity of the student body and the faculty. In his brief tenure as dean, Charles Burnette hired Michael Benedikt, Larry Doll, Michael Garrison, and Larry Speck. This foursome has provided a diverse intellectual core for the past four decades.

Looking forward, with more than half of the world's population living in metropolitan regions, opportunities abound for the design and planning disciplines in this first urban century. Urbanization is expected to continue to increase globally through the twenty-first century. Clearly, many urban areas are failures by almost any measure—social, economic, environmental, energy efficiency, or aesthetic.

The global built environment needs to be redesigned. We should strive to make buildings, landscapes, and cities more conserving, more resilient, and more beautiful. This will require considerable imagination.

Architecture, design, and planning education challenges students to imagine the future. Design is a creative act, where the ending point is unknown at the start. Looking forward to the next hundred years, we know that imagination can only be realized by knowledge. As a result, research will play an ever important role in design and planning education. Interdisciplinary research is especially significant; it is work that brings together design and planning, engineering and history, ecology and art. The global reach and consequences of this research will be increasingly essential.

Our School of Architecture and The University of Texas at Austin are well-positioned to respond to the challenges of the future. We have a solid foundation, an essential building block for any construction. We possess the human capital—bright students, accomplished faculty, generous friends and alumni, dedicated staff—to advance our disciplines. We already offer strong programs in Europe, Latin America, and Asia. The University of Texas at Austin possesses an amazing can-do spirit.

After I moved to Texas, I met many individuals who embody this spirit, but in particular I found it in three remarkable women who advanced our appreciation of architecture, civic activism, and environmentalism. All three also had a profound impact on our school. The first is Lady Bird Johnson, who played a central role in the environmental movement of the 1960s and 1970s and did much to preserve historic monuments and landscapes in Texas. She founded the Lady Bird Johnson Wildflower Center, which is now part of the School of Architecture and the College of Natural Science.

The second is Dallas philanthropist Margaret McDermott who has done much to advance art and architecture in her hometown and state. She is playing a central role in establishing the Trinity River Corridor Project and the bridges designed by Santiago Calatrava spanning the river. Mrs. McDermott has also established the Eugene McDermott Visiting Professorship, the Margaret McDermott Centennial Teaching Fellowship in Architecture, and the Eugene and Margaret McDermott Excellence Fund for the Study of Architecture.

The third is Ruth Carter Stevenson who built the Amon Carter Museum in Fort Worth after her father's death in 1955, engaging Philip Johnson in the original design and two additions. Her own home was designed in 1956 by Harwell Hamilton Harris following his resignation as director of the School of Architecture. She is fond of

the house and equally so of her garden, designed by the California modern landscape architect Tommy Church. Mrs. Stevenson also endowed a chair in the school devoted to American architecture and architectural history. This chair has enabled us to bring numerous luminaries to Austin.

In my first contact with Mrs. Stevenson, I had a potentially risky proposition. We were beginning our Master of Landscape Architecture program, and I was considering inviting Laurie Olin to be our Ruth Carter Stevenson Chair. Although educated as an architect, he practices landscape architecture. I called Mrs. Stevenson with the proposition.

"He's perfect!" She responded, "We worked together on the National Gallery of Art Sculpture Garden, and I adore the man."

In addition, Mrs. Stevenson chose to involve Olin in the design of a children's garden at the Forth Worth Botanic Gardens. Eventually, she also engaged him in the redesign of Lawrence Halprin's Heritage Plaza in Fort Worth's Heritage Park. Mrs. Stevenson observed, "This is a park that celebrates our city's history, standing on the site where the city was first settled."

This trio of Texas women—Johnson, McDermott, and Stevenson—exhibits profound vision, amazing generosity, and considerable spunk. They recognize the value of higher education generally and design and planning education more specifically.

The value of higher education to economic well-being was certainly recognized by Texas' founders, who in the state constitution, included the goal to establish a "university of the first class," which became The University of Texas at Austin. To remain a university of the first class, we need need people—students, faculty, alumni, staff, and friends—of the highest caliber to create a better living environment for future generations.

[1] Kurt Lewin. *Field Theory in Social Science; Selected Theoretical Papers*. D. Cartwright, ed. (New York: Harper & Row, 1951), 169.

Introduction

Richard L. Cleary, Professor, Page Southerland Page Fellow in Architecture. Faculty member since 1995.

The University of Texas at Austin took a decisive step in its support of the profession of architecture with its appointment in 1910 of Hugo F. Kuehne as professor in the College of Engineering's new bachelor's program in architecture. This was not the first degree in architecture offered in Texas. That distinction was earned five years earlier by Texas A&M University, but from the outset, UT sought to distinguish itself from its rival on the Brazos. While both programs were units within engineering colleges, the bachelor of science in architecture offered by UT implied somewhat more disciplinary independence than A&M's bachelor of science in architectural engineering. For Kuehne, architecture was a fine art. In a manifesto published in 1911, he defined architecture as "the art of *conceiving* and *creating* buildings which are to serve the *uses of mankind* in the most *usable*, *durable*, and *expressive* form."[1] [his italics] Kuehne may have pushed his agenda too hard, because a year later he was replaced as head by Frederick E. Giesecke, who had founded the architecture program at A&M and would eventually return to College Station after leading UT's department for fifteen years. During his service in Austin, Giesecke found a balance between the fine arts approach and engineering. The School of Architecture (its official designation as school or department has changed over the years) retained a distinction between architecture and architectural engineering as separate degree programs, and was the center on campus for the study of drawing and watercolor.

If Kuehne and Giesecke could return to campus today, they would still be able to orient themselves on the Forty Acres with reference to buildings they knew in the 1910s despite the university's growth over the past century. The first home of the School of Architecture, the former Engineering Building (now the Gebauer Building), still stands (thanks to the efforts of architecture faculty member Dan Leary in the 1990s), and Battle Hall, which they knew as the University Library, remains a library, now devoted exclusively to collections on architecture and planning that exceed the total number of volumes the university owned when the building opened in 1911. Sutton Hall for them was the Education Building, and Giesecke, who was teaching at the time of its construction (Kuehne was in private practice), likely urged his students to take note of its reinforced-concrete frame, an emerging technology in 1917.

Both men would certainly appreciate Goldsmith Hall, which opened in 1933 as a purpose-built structure for architectural education, and we might be surprised by how well they could follow the curricula of our professional degree programs in architecture. In his manifesto, Kuehne divided the architecture curriculum into four areas of study: technique (visual communication in our terminology), composition and design (simply labeled "design" today), history (architectural and social), and construction and practice (equivalent to our construction, environmental controls, and professional practice sequences). While some methods of instruction have changed, the task of guiding students to create meaningful forms through a creative synthesis of technical and cultural factors remains central to school's mission, just as it was one hundred years ago.

Awareness of such continuities inspired the faculty when we first discussed ways of marking the School of Architecture's centenary. Wilfried Wang found the phrase, "Traces and Trajectories," that became the theme for the centennial-year activities. It recognizes the importance of revisiting the school's history, of not taking the present for granted, and of speculating about the future. The faculty also indicated a preference for activities that would offer opportunities for multiple voices to reflect on their experiences as students, staff, and faculty and declare their aspirations for the next hundred years. That mandate has shaped this book.

The traces and trajectories presented in these pages do well in describing the School of Architecture as a tapestry composed of many disciplines that simultaneously maintain their professional identities and are integral to the whole. More difficult to convey are the individual efforts, perseverance, and, even, acts of intellectual bravery that underlie curricular innovation, research, and design in the school. Usually, the accompanying feelings of frustration and exhilaration are unrecorded and are shared only among family and friends, but there have been cases in the school's history when circumstances have required more public expression.

Hal Box's essay recalls the now legendary encounter of Dean Alan Taniguchi and the chairman of the Board of Regents, Frank Erwin, in 1969 when the dean refused Erwin's order that he take action against the architecture students who were protesting the removal of trees along Waller Creek to make room for the expansion of the stadium. Taniguchi's principled refusal on behalf of his students and the environment was but one episode in a larger struggle in which he and other academic leaders fought with the powerful regent over the soul of the university.[2] His battle ended three years later, in April 1972, when he resigned to become director of the architecture program at Rice University. After Erwin claimed that the resignation was merely over a dispute concerning Taniguchi's professional practice and went on to invite the departure of the rest of the architecture faculty and, while he was at it, of the history faculty, too ("It would give us a chance to start over and develop some fine departments"), Taniguchi responded publicly with his own explanation. "The University teaching-learning environment has rapidly deteriorated into a climate of distrust at the expense of a quality education for the student," he wrote, and he then described how he could no longer in good conscience play his role in an administrative hierarchy that had forsaken teachers and students for football and executive office buildings.[3] Taniguchi's departure did not lead to changes overnight, but it contributed to reassessments that gradually improved the intellectual climate on campus.

Twenty-seven years after Taniguchi's dramatic resignation, Dean Larry Speck encountered a situation involving the Board of Regents in which he, too, found it necessary to step down from his position as a matter of principle. His action in November 1999 came a week after Herzog & de Meuron Architekten resigned the commission to design the Blanton Museum of Art.[4] The issue for Speck was the regents' failure both to respect the architect selection process and to treat the winning firm professionally. His resignation, like Taniguchi's, was not intended to force a particular outcome as much as to draw attention to problems that he could not overlook. In addition to the matter of the regents' treatment of the architects and, also, the representatives of the Austin campus, Speck emphasized the need to regard Cesar Pelli's campus master plan as a framework open to creative interpretation rather than as a rigid formula for building red-tiled boxes.

The stands taken by Taniguchi and Speck reflect the degree to which the tapestry of the School of Architecture is woven into the larger fabric of the university and of the professions in which the school's alumni and faculty practice. The following essays and Traces demonstrate how this is done on campus, in Austin, in Texas, across the nation, and around the world.

The essays are loosely grouped by thematic affinity, framed by David Heymann's paean to Goldsmith Hall and Eric Hepburn's reflection on time, which sweep us in and out of our topic like the famous zoom shots of the universe in the short film by Charles and Ray Eames, *Powers of Ten* (1968). Among the essays, Traces highlight aspects of the school's history. These might be thought of as trailers for essays that have yet to be written chronicling the people and ideas that have passed through the school. Pursuing these topics requires patient mining of the archival collections of the university's administrative records, faculty papers, and student projects deposited in the Alexander Architectural Archive and the Dolph Briscoe Center for American History.

The final section of the book consists of two portfolios. The first presents examples of student work from every decade of the school's history. The second portfolio presents work by alumni exhibited in the school's Mebane Gallery in November 2010.

Besides the authors of the essays and work illustrated in the Traces and portfolios, many people have contributed to this book, the production of which has been made possible by the generosity of the Amon G. Carter Foundation. In 2008, Dean Steiner formed an advisory committee of faculty and alumni to help frame the scope of the book: Miroslava Benes, Kent Butler, Elizabeth

Danze, Terry Kahn, Reed Kroloff, Nancy Kwallek, John McRae, Talia McCray, Larry Speck, Richard Swallow, and Wilfried Wang. Graduate research assistants expanded on the pioneering work on the school's history that Lila Stillson had begun in the 1980s and located historic photographs and student work: Samuel Dodd, Emily Freeman, Elise King, Laura McGuire, Kate Murphy, Kathryn Pierce, and Diana Su. I owe a great debt to my colleagues who shared their knowledge of the school with me, especially Richard Swallow, my former neighbor in Sutton Hall, who taught in the school for fifty years. Our research was facilitated by the skill and patience of Margaret Schlankey and her staff at the Dolph Briscoe Center for American History and of the staff of the Architecture and Planning Library and Alexander Architectural Archive: Beth Dodd, Martha

González Palacios, Daniel Orozco, Donna Coates, and Nancy Sparrow. In addition to Dean Steiner, other members of the school's administration who provided assistance and kept the project on track include Jeanne Crawford, Amy Crossette, Jeff Evelyn, Rosemin Gopaul, Julie Hooper, Garrett Loontjer, Christine Marcin, Pamela Peters, Elizabeth Shaub, and the indefatigable Stacy Manning. Cameron Kraus created the distinctive look of this book and cheerfully found harmonious arrangements for the texts and images Samuel Dodd and Elise King, my assistant editors, and I sent his way. Christine Wong brought calm and experience as production editor. Sarah Cleary guided researchers at the Briscoe Center, lent her eyes to the review of the manuscript, and her ears to my woes and successes.

[1] Hugo Franz Kuehne, "Academic Training in Architecture," *Bulletin of the University of Texas*, no. 176 (22 March 1911), 3-33.

[2] For an introduction to these controversies, see Richard A. Holland, "Thirteen Ways of Looking at Chairman Frank," in Richard A. Holland, ed., *The Texas Book* (Austin: University of Texas Press, 2006), 53-72.

[3] Frank Erwin's comments were reported in the press. See "Of Beer and Barbecue Talk," *The Daily Texan* (28 April 1972). For Alan Taniguchi's statement, see Alan Y. Taniguchi, "Taniguchi's Explanation," *The Daily Texan* (4 May 1972).

[4] The Blanton story was widely reported locally and in the national architectural press. For a thoughtful account, see Mark W. Gunderson, "A Flaw in the System: A Battle over Architecture Strips the University of Texas of a Signature Building," *Cite: The Architecture and Design Review of Houston*, 47 (Spring 2000), 34-37.

Above: Architecture
Students, 1915,
clockwise from top
left: W.G. Stacy,
Thomas D. Broad,
Stella T. Elmendorf,
and Nellie
Jefferson

Right: Hugo Kuehne
(bottom row,
center) and the
Brush and Pencil
Club, 1913

EARLY GRADUATES

BERTRAM GIESECKE (1892-1950), the son of Professor Frederick Giesecke, became the school's first graduate in 1913. After World War I, he founded the firm of Giesecke and Harris, which remained in practice in Austin until 1941. The firm produced Austin's prominent neo-gothic skyscraper, the Norwood Tower (1929). Giesecke served as consulting architect for the U.S. Treasury Department (1935) and chairman of the Texas Relief Commission (1933-34).

THE CLASS OF 1915

THOMAS BROAD (1893-1985) designed many commercial structures in Dallas over his career and some farming communities as part of Depression-era relief efforts. He served on the State Board of Architectural Examiners (1937-1951), the board of directors of the Dallas Museum of Art, and the Dallas Council on World Affairs.

STELLA "TEXAS" ELMENDORF-TYLOR (1885-1980) was a native of San Antonio. Prior to her enrollment at UT, she studied painting with Robert Henri in New York. Upon graduation, she briefly worked at UT as an architectural draftsperson and instructor before moving to the Midwest where she painted and taught art.

WILLIAM HENRY LIGHTFOOT (1892-1985) received a post-graduate degree from Harvard University. He worked in partnership with Townes, Lightfoot, & Funk in Amarillo. The firm designed the Porter County Courthouse (1931). From 1940 to 1960, he practiced in Paris, Texas, designing numerous educational buildings.

NELLIE JEFFERSON (1886-1955) assisted in research for the Division of Engineering in the Bureau of Economic Geology and Technology. Like many subsequent UT graduates, she went to MIT for advanced study, receiving a MS in Architecture in 1921.

Members of
the BArch
graduating
class, 2010

CENTENNIAL CLASS

The School of Architecture's centennial-year graduating class of 2010 numbered 128 men and women from Texas, other regions of the United States, and from around the world. Approximately half earned undergraduate professional degrees in architecture and interior design or completed the bachelor of architectural studies program. The graduate-degree recipients represented the school's broad offerings, which include professional degrees in community and regional planning, architecture, and landscape architecture; academic master's degrees in historic preservation, architectural history, sustainable design, urban design, and architectural studies; and PhD programs in community and regional planning, architectural history, and historic preservation.

Like the class of 1915, which faced an uncertain future as the nation struggled to recover from economic recession, adjusted to modernization, and debated its role in a global war, the members of the centennial class have begun their professional careers at a challenging time. They face a slow economy and a highly competitive job market, urgent social and environmental issues, and transformations in professional practice. But the class of 2010 has opportunities that were unavailable to their predecessors. Although women constituted half of the school's first graduating class, their career options in architecture were limited. Even more formidable barriers based on race and ethnicity blocked access for many people to higher education and the professions. The measure of the School of Architecture's success today is how well it has prepared its graduates to view change as opportunity and to act on the motto of the University of Texas at Austin: what starts here changes the world.

The Early Years

ARCHITECTURE AT THE UNIVERSITY OF TEXAS

As at many American universities, architectural instruction at the University of Texas began in the College of Engineering. Yet, in a 1912 letter to UT President Mezes, founding professor Hugo Kuehne described the two-year-old School of Architecture as "an absolutely new departure, a new creation, with its peculiar character, its individuality and dissimilarity." Kuehne faced a number of challenges in establishing the program, which had over thirty registered students for classes in 1912. He felt that public taste needed to be cultivated, instilling an appreciation for architectural aesthetics and stimulating a supportive artistic environment. The new school required a reputable faculty, separate working spaces, equipment, and materials, including a library and lantern slide collection. Even in the face of such challenges, Kuehne prophetically observed that "it is beyond question that the School of Architecture will fill a great need in this state, and the forecast is encouraging."

Over the next two decades, the school expanded under the seasoned leadership of Frederick Giesecke and Goldwin Goldsmith. New faculty included Samuel Gideon, Raymond Everett, Robert L. White (who also served as UT's supervising architect), Samuel Vosper, and Walter Rolfe. In 1925, the school became the first in Texas to be accepted for membership in the Association of Collegiate Schools of Architecture. The five-year Bachelor of Architecture degree was established in 1930 and accreditation by the National Architectural Accreditation Board followed in 1935. The school moved into its permanent home in the Architecture Building (Goldsmith Hall) in 1933.

HUGO F. KUEHNE (1884-1963) was the first professor of architecture at the University of Texas. An Austin native, Kuehne received his bachelor's degree in civil engineering from UT in 1906 and a bachelor's degree in architecture from MIT in 1908. After returning to UT in 1910, Kuehne created the first curriculum for the School of Architecture within the College of Engineering. His efforts to create a Beaux-Arts design-based curriculum caused tension with supporters of the engineering curriculum in the college. Kuehne left UT in 1914 and established his professional practice in Austin, working as a principal with several firms until his retirement in 1961. He served as president of the Austin Chapter of the AIA in 1944. One of his notable buildings is the Austin Public Library (1933), now the Austin History Center.

FREDERICK E. GIESECKE (1869-1953), a Texas Aggie turned Longhorn, was the school's chairman from 1912 to 1927. The Texas-born architect received his bachelor's degree in mechanical engineering from A&M in 1886, an architecture degree from MIT in 1904, and a PhD from the University of Illinois in 1924. Following his studies at MIT, Giesecke began his teaching career at College Station, where he developed the curriculum in architectural engineering. He later returned to A&M after his fifteen years of service in Austin. UT's architecture program advanced significantly during his tenure. He enlarged the faculty, increased the department's budget, and restructured the curriculum. Starting in 1913, the school offered courses in descriptive geometry, business practice, and constructive design, complementing Kuehne's Beaux-Arts-inspired drawing sequence.

GOLDWIN GOLDSMITH (1871-1962) was appointed chairman in 1928. Like many of his generation, he had begun his career as a draftsman, working for McKim, Mead, and White from 1888-1890. He then pursued formal studies at Columbia University, earning a PhD in architecture 1896. After a year in Paris polishing his design skills in the atelier of Jean-Henry Duray, a professor at the Ecole des Beaux-Arts, Goldsmith opened a firm in New York with Joseph Van Vleck. In 1913, the University of Kansas named him director of its new architecture program. At this time, Goldsmith also was a co-founder of the recently established Association of Collegiate Schools of Architecture. He came to UT fifteen years later with nationally recognized experience in architectural education and a clear agenda for securing accreditation for its professional degree program. Goldsmith's course on specifications was a favorite of students, and he authored a standard textbook on the subject in 1935. Goldsmith resigned as chairman in 1935 but continued teaching until 1955, a beloved figure in the school for whom the Architecture Building was named in 1978.

At its inception, the School of Architecture offered the first fine arts curriculum at the University of Texas and remained the center for the study of painting and drawing until the late 1920s. The university catalog described architecture as a fine art, requiring broad training in design and composition, aesthetic culture, and the principles of sound construction. The approach reflected Kuehne's training at MIT, which was inspired by the pedagogy of the Ecole des Beaux-Arts in Paris, the gold standard of architectural education at the turn of the twentieth century. The early curriculum reveals the school's struggle to balance this vision with the applied practices of the College of Engineering. The four-year BS in Architecture began with two years of preparatory studies in mathematics, science, and drawing before the first architectural design studio.

Above: Alma Giesecke (BS '17), A Drinking Fountain: Sophomore Year, 1914

Right: Edward Fritz Ries (BS '16), Charcoal Drawing: Sophomore Year, 1914

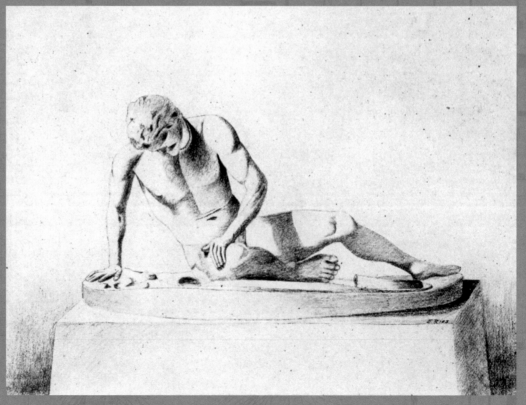

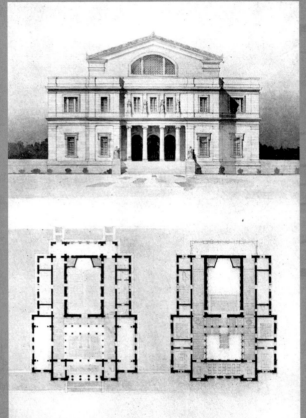

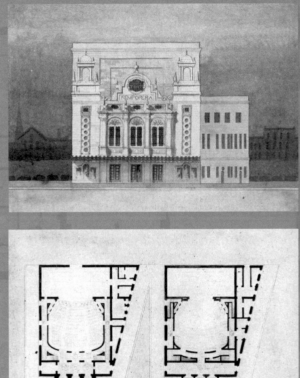

Left: Stella T. Elmendorf (BS '15), A Building to Serve as a Social Center: Senior Year, Architectural Design, 1914/1915

Right: Paul Preston Brooks (BS '16), project for a theater: Junior Year, Architectural Design, 1915

Stella T. Elmendorf (BS '15), A Catholic Church:
Senior Year, Architectural Design, 1914/1915

CURRICULUM, 1911/1912
Bachelor of Science in Architecture (4 Years)

FIRST YEAR

Fall Term
Trigonometry
English 1
Chemistry 1
Surveying
Elementary Mechanical Drawing
First Year Freehand Drawing

Winter Term
Algebra
English 1
Analytics
Chemistry 1
Elementary Mechanical Drawing
First Year Freehand Drawing

Spring Term
Algebra
English 1
Analytics
Chemistry 1
Elementary Mechanical Drawing
First Year Freehand Drawing

SECOND YEAR

Fall Term
Calculus
English 2
Physics 1
Elements of Architecture
Descriptive Geometries
Second Year Freehand Drawing
Architectural History

Winter Term
Calculus
Physics 1
English 2
Elements of Architecture
Shades and Shadows/Perspective
Second Year Freehand Drawing
Architectural History

Spring Term
Calculus
Physics 1
English 2
Elements of Architecture
Mechanics
Second Year Freehand Drawing
Architectural History

THIRD YEAR

Fall Term
Third Year Design
Applied Mechanics
Architectural History
Third Year Freehand Drawing
Pen and Pencil
History of Ornament
French A

Winter Term
Third Year Design
Applied Mechanics
Architectural History
Third Year Freehand Drawing
Pen and Pencil
History of Ornament
French A

Spring Term
Third Year Design
Theory of Architecture
Architectural History
Third Year Freehand Drawing
Water Color
History of Ornament
French A

FOURTH YEAR

Fall Term
Fourth Year Design
Fourth Year Freehand Drawing
Building Construction
Constructive Design
French 1
Economics

Winter Term
Fourth Year Design
Fourth Year Freehand Drawing
Building Construction
Constructive Design
Heating and Ventilation
French 1
Economics

Spring Term
Fourth Year Design
Fourth Year Freehand Drawing
Building Construction
Constructive Design
French 1
Economics

Kayla Lyssy (BArch '10), Bayou St. John Learning Center:
Advanced Design, Angelo Bucci, critic, 2010

CURRICULUM , 2010/2012
Bachelor of Architecture (5 Years)

FIRST YEAR

Fall Term
Design 1
Visual Communication 1
Architecture and Society
Rhetoric and Composition
Calculus 1

Spring Term
Design 2
Visual Communication 2
History of Architecture 1
General Physics 1
Physics Laboratory 1
First-Year Signature Course

SECOND YEAR

Fall Term
Design 3
Visual Communication 3
History of Architecture 2
Construction 1
General Physics 2
Physics Laboratory 2

Spring Term
Design 4
Topics in History of Architecture
Construction 2
Masterworks of Literature
Site Design

THIRD YEAR

Fall Term
Design 5
Environmental Controls 1
Construction 3
American History
Social Science Elective

Spring Term
Design 6
Construction 4
Environmental Controls 2
Liberal Arts Elective

Portfolio Review

FOURTH YEAR

Fall Term
Advanced Design
American Government
American History
Humanities Elective
Natural Science Elective

Spring Term
Advanced Design
Technical Communication
American Government
Construction 5
Principles of Planning

FIFTH YEAR

Fall Term
Advanced Design
Topics in History of Architecture
Liberal Arts Elective
Open Elective
Open Elective

Spring Term
Advanced Design
Professional Practice
Topics in History of Architecture
Liberal Arts Elective
Open Elective

Buildings: Searching for a Home

As a new department within the College of Engineering, Architecture did not have a permanent home of its own for over twenty years. Space was often limited and some of its early locations were less than desirable. In 1911, the first architecture courses were housed in the university Power Plant. Above the boiler room and engineering workshops, Professor Kuehne led architecture students in freehand drawing exercises. The heat and noise made for a challenging work environment, forcing him to request more suitable quarters the following year.

The program relocated to the second floor of the Old Engineering Building (now the Gebauer Building), but students also traveled to the top floor of Old Main Building to study and draw the plaster casts of ancient classical sculpture and architectural details assembled by Professor William J. Battle. Enrollment continued to grow, and by 1919, Architecture was the second largest department within Engineering.

The department moved again in 1927 taking over three floors of B hall, the former men's dormitory. The main floor housed the library and drafting rooms with offices and classrooms in the wings. The third floor followed a similar plan, but had another drafting room instead of a library. The top floor was much smaller and was used for freehand drawing classes. At first, B Hall's space seemed more than adequate, but it soon became evident that a building dedicated solely to architecture was necessary. In 1929, enrollment ballooned to 216 students. Within several years, studios spilled out into hallways and the library was often standing room only. In the fall of 1930, the Department of Architecture submitted a request for a building of its own.

Exhibit of student work, Drafting Room, Engineering Building (now Gebauer Building), ca. 1916

Engineering Building with the Power Plant (on site of Welch Hall, demolished 1977) visible in the background

Left: Sophomore Drafting Room, B. Hall, 1927

Bottom Left: Floorplan showing the Department of Architecture in B. Hall, 1927

Bottom Right: B. Hall in 1927 (demolished 1952). It stood to the east of Main Building.

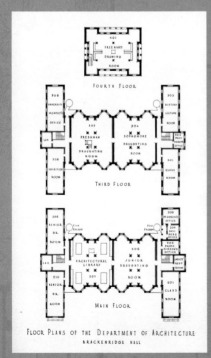

FLOOR PLANS OF THE DEPARTMENT OF ARCHITECTURE
BRACKENRIDGE HALL

Completed in 1933, the Architecture Building was designed specifically for the teaching of architecture. Led by Goldwin Goldsmith, for whom the building was renamed in 1978, the faculty worked closely with Consulting Architect Paul Cret, Supervising Architect and Professor Robert Leon White (BS '1921, MS 1930), and Dallas architects Hebert M. Greene, LaRoche & Dahl. Its facilities included well-lit studios framing a courtyard and oriented to the prevailing breeze, a second-floor library, and specialized areas such as a cubicle-filled room where the students worked individually *en loge* to develop their *partis* for Beaux-Arts design projects and, in the tower, a room where muralists could practice their art. With the Texas Union, the building holds a key position in Cret's 1933 master development plan marking the entrance to the busy West Mall.

Above:
Raymond Everett,
Architecture Building
(Goldsmith Hall),
1932

Bottom Left:
Goldsmith Hall
Courtyard

Top Right:
Architecture
Building studio

Bottom Right:
Architecture Building
(Goldsmith Hall),
1933

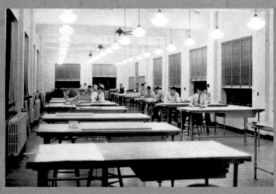

Left: Goldsmith Hall expansion and renovation, 1987

Below: Design Lab (Woodshop) in Goldsmith Hall, 2010

In the 1970s and 1980s, the school once again needed to improve its facilities. Not only had its programs outgrown Goldsmith Hall, but changes were needed to keep up new technologies in architectural practice and education. Dean Charles Burnette secured the transfer of the library to Battle Hall in 1973, and Dean Hal Box subsequently expanded the school's presence there and in Sutton Hall and led renovations of Sutton and Goldsmith Halls, designed by Thomas, Booziotis and Associates.

Bill Booziotis's (BArch '57) work on Goldsmith Hall added a three-story addition to the south of the original building providing additional review spaces, a lecture hall, offices, and the woodshop. He also fixed previous renovation attempts to reassert the building's original character, which he elegantly respected in the addition.

Buildings: A Campus within a Campus

SUTTON HALL

Above: Sutton Hall, south facade, 2007

Right: Reading Room, Architecture and Planning Library, Battle Hall, 2010

Below: Battle Hall, east facade, 2010

Today, the School of Architecture occupies a tightly-knit group of four buildings. In addition to Goldsmith Hall, they include Battle Hall, Sutton Hall, and portions of the West Mall Office Building.

Designed by Cass Gilbert, Battle Hall was built in 1911 to serve as the university library. It currently houses the Alexander Architectural Archive, the Architecture and Planning Library, and the Center for American Architecture and Design.

Gilbert also designed Sutton Hall, completed in 1918, which housed the School of Education. Booziotis's renovation in 1982 adapted it for Architecture. In addition to studios and faculty offices, it houses the computer lab, graduate programs office, Visual Resources Collection, and the Career Services Center.

The West Mall Office Building is the most recent addition to the school's campus. Designed to house administrative offices by Jessen, Jessen, Millhouse and Greeven along with Staub, Rather and Howze, it was built in 1960 on a site Paul Cret's master plan of 1933 had reserved for a university museum connected to Battle Hall. Although it lacks the architectural distinction of its neighbors, it has a prime location and space to accommodate such School of Architecture facilities as the University Co-op Materials Resource Center, the Conservation Lab, the Thermal Lab, the Center of Sustainable Development, and faculty offices.

Despite their proximity and overall architectural quality, the school's buildings pose a number of challenges for the future. Space for students, faculty, staff, equipment, and collections remains tight and is often compartmentalized, which can work against the open communication that is such an important part of architectural education, research, and practice. In 2007, David Heymann, Barbara Hoidn, and Wilfried Wang explored ways of reorganizing the distribution of activities within the architecture campus to facilitate interaction among the design studios, to make events such as exhibitions and reviews more visible, and to concentrate the school's information resources in Battle Hall, which would be renovated to open internal connections to the West Mall Office Building and beyond to the Goldsmith courtyard.

Left: Materials Lab, West Mall Building, 2010

Below: Ferris Wheel Installation, West Mall Building, 1999

Study for the reorganization of the architecture campus, David Heymann, Barbara Hoidn, and Wilfried Wang, 2007

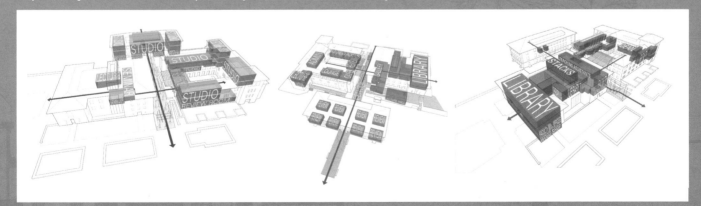

I ♥ Goldsmith Hall

David Heymann, The Martin S. Kermacy Centennial Professor in Architecture, Distinguished Teaching Professor. Faculty member since 1991.

THE ROUGH DIAGONAL of the Balcones Escarpment through Central Texas neatly divides a land of rock from a land of soil. West, on the Edwards Plateau, the high limestone hills, sparse with stunted live oak, are at best discretely top-soiled, while bald cypress grows along the clear shallow riverbeds. The bedrock is fossil bearing, once the shore and shallows of a great Paleozoic ocean. A century ago this splendid region, the Hill Country, was perhaps the poorest in the nation: a common profession was making charcoal from Ashe juniper, commonly known as cedar. The Hill Country has been suitable for tribal hunting, limited subsistence farming, and big ranching. Today, given the collapse of the cattle economy but the splendor of the setting, it's suitable mostly for retiring. East of the escarpment are the rolling Blackland Prairies, named for their rich varied soils composed in part by the erosion of that primeval shore as the water level of the sea fell. These were literally continental mud flats. Richly forested with live, Spanish, and water oaks, as well as elm, walnut, and pecan, the Blacklands generously supported hunting and gathering, farming, and drilling for oil and gas. You can imagine early settlers' doubt, having—on their irrevocable push west—bypassed this fertile plain only to confront the barren uplift. Damn. Gone too far.

A wonderful sequence of rivers—the Frio, the Medina, Sabinal, San Antonio, Guadalupe, Blanco, Comal,

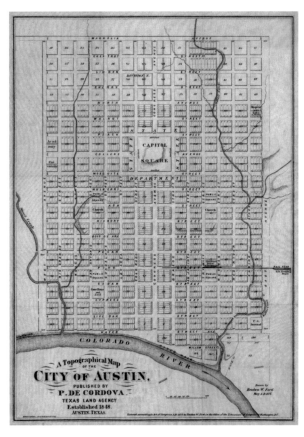

Colorado—sutures these two landscapes together. Interstate 35 is scar tissue along the cut. San Antonio, San Marcos, New Braunfels, Austin, Temple, Waco —even Dallas—are successively situated where the next river brings clear limestone filtered water to workable land. The abruptness of the faulted escarpment, conspiring with the high water table of the plateau's immense aquifer, blesses each of these cities with abundant, legendary springs: Barton Springs (Austin), Comal Springs (New Braunfels), the San Marcos springs (now an eco-park, but once called Aquarena Springs, home to Ralph the swimming pig), the Eden of San Antonio's Brackenridge Park, where water wells up biblically in the rocky zoo. So, for portentous geologic reasons, it makes sense to site a city where Austin is. The location has been inhabited for at least 12,000 years—early European settlers founded a hamlet here named Waterloo. The city we call Austin came into being as an act of political will, like Madrid, Mexico City, or Brasília. Debate on where to locate a new Texas capital raged following nationhood in 1836. Ultimately, a neutral location central to the territory, though at the edge of what was then settled, was favored. This symbolic gesture was also pragmatic: the center lay conveniently above the yellow-fevered coastal plain. Mirabeau Lamar headed the siting commission. Legend holds he'd already decided on the location while hunting buffalo the year before, and Waterloo was quickly deemed appropriate to the young nation's desire. This desire can be reasonably inferred from the character of the landscape chosen. Two parallel creeks—Shoal, Waller—run south into the eastward

flowing Colorado, framing a group of prominent hills, each a great south-facing slope of wildflowers, waist-high grass, and live oak motts: all propitious feng shui, all good with Vitruvius.

Between the two streams and the river a simple grid was platted centered on the first great hilltop at about the intersection of Congress Avenue and College (now 12th) Street, where four blocks were combined as the site for the new capitol building. In name, the north-south avenues identified, east to west, the rivers of Texas, while the east-west streets specified the trees found here. If a Platonic order was thus laid over an Aristotelian landscape in a nearly perfect intersection of symbolic cosmology and actual geography, these were not in fact so dissimilar, since the ideal was merely a map of the real. It may be a coincidence that the illumination of Austin's first street lights—thirty-one 150-foot high towers—reminded its inhabitants of moonlight, but it is certainly meaningful that more than half of these century-old towers still operate, having long been extirpated in cities lacking the necessary sensitivities. Of course the Austin that exists today is

Left: *Tectonic Map of Texas*, from T. E. Ewing, *The Tectonic Framework of Texas*, 1990

Right: *Topographical Map of the City of Austin*, 1872, cartographer Rueban W. Ford

not exactly as planned. The cross streets—the great map of trees—are now numbered. If legibility of way finding has been gained, another legibility has been lost. But — a radical improvement to the plan—The University of Texas was relocated from its subservient placement on the cross axis to a position of greater geographical prominence, crowning the second great hill up from the river. In the long north-south section of the city —variously visible as you enter Austin—it claims equal stature to the Capitol. Like Austin, the university's plan and cosmology are dictated by the intersection of an ideal map and geographic circumstance. In Paul Cret's masterful design, the campus is ordered by cross-axial pedestrian malls, each named for the direction it leads from the hilltop site of the Library (now the Main Building), the iconic Tower of which housed book stacks, a solid complement to the empty capitol dome. One startling quality of the Tower— perversely sited off the east-west axis and, because of its short floor-to-floor height, difficult to read in scale — is that it hovers over the campus without being readily locatable. Another perceptual dilemma of Cret's design is that, while the tree-lined malls divide the original campus into distinct quadrants, these are less clear in experience. This is a consequence of the underlying sectional topography of the campus: shelf-like east-west terraces dropping primarily southward (toward the capitol) and eastward from the central hilltop. Here, practical circulation is east and west, while motion north and south is portentous, a fact cleverly recognized in Cret's 1933

Detail, 1933 Plan of Development, The University of Texas, Paul Cret, Consulting Architect

master plan. Larger programmatic changes are thus perceived moving north and south, and, indeed, the North Mall slams quickly into the gates of Mary Gearing Hall—start of what was once the Women's Campus— while the South Mall, dropping rapidly, telescopes the eye to the dome of the Capitol in the middle distance. From the steps of Main Building and the grand South Terrace before it, our commencement speakers, our students, professors, administrators, our graduates and their families, our slackers and passersby, all are given pause to consider the Capitol and the workings that it houses. A more perfect, more devious subject for such a view could hardly be devised.

If the large order of Cret's master plan is typologically similar, in miniature, to that of Austin—cross axes within a bounded field, centered on, and rising to, a dominant site and program—a difference occurs at the intermediate scale of organization. While movement along the malls is clear, movement from the malls is less so, as the plan abruptly gives way from large-scale lucidity to small-scale privacy in support of a change in program from crowded malls to quiet courtyards— from circulation to the accomplishments of study (this consideration in Cret's design is well described in Carol McMichael's *Paul Cret at Texas*).[1] Cret's Architecture Building—now Goldsmith Hall—evidences this dual nature powerfully. Goldsmith is situated where the West Mall intersects Guadalupe Street, one of two primary entries to the university. Cret embedded a four-story tower into Goldsmith's three-story West Mall facade that mirrors a similar tower embedded in the Texas Union across the mall, forming a gateway the architect studied with care. Seen from the mall, this tower is pushed with abrupt violence into the soft fleshiness of an otherwise workmanlike elevation. Yet within Goldsmith, this dramatic formal element has negligible effect. Off axis, unaligned with the ground floor hallway, it is, like the Tower, there but not locatable. The West Mall is lost from view immediately, almost before one finds the courtyard. This courtyard, facing east, rather than north to the West Mall, of course perfectly realigns Goldsmith with the symbolic axis of the South Terrace—though the pergola and change in elevation aid in masking this relationship. Thus rendered empty yet fraught, the courtyard is a private space masquerading as a public forum, the perfect subject for consideration by the young architect looking up from his or her work in doubt.

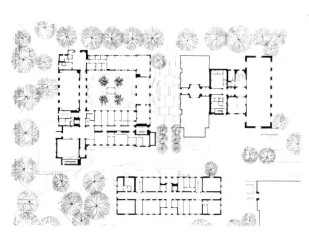

The true mark of the architect's skill is a conspiracy of the technical and cultural. The courtyard—so perfectly, so subtly and surprisingly defined—allows Goldsmith to take advantage of prevailing breezes and exposures while reducing the onslaught of western sun. The section of the studio wings reflects this knowledge in the vastly increased dimension of north-facing windows. The symmetric alignment of the courtyard with respect to the honorific east-west axis of the university is thus tempered by an equally fundamental but asymmetrical north-south alignment to wind and sun. Standing in the courtyard, at first you really do not notice the startling size of the north-facing windows—and the attendant asymmetry—because these are perpetually in shade. But once you see it—like that arrow in FedEx—you will never again miss this balanced imbalance of natural and institutional. It is through one of these immense windows that my office surveys the world. From it, I see diagonally across the courtyard to the Tower. While I cannot see the Capitol, I know, nonetheless, that the Tower is engaged in debate with the dome, which, in turn, is located with definitive regard to the state and nation. So I can, from my office, indeed from this table at which I am proofreading, look up and quite easily engage myself, by projection, in the whole of an extraordinary structure (the cosmology of Texas!), itself a series of orders, each perfectly nested one within the other moving out in scale from this sheet of paper to the geologic. To that end, I have successfully moved bookcases in front of the window in my office door (looking into the corridor), to stifle a little distraction that was threatening my deep and abiding love for Goldsmith Hall.

Left: Study for Renovation of the School of Architecture Buildings

Right: View of The Tower from Goldsmith Hall

[1] Carol McMichael, *Paul Cret at Texas: Architectural Drawing and the Image of the University in the 1930s* (Austin: Archer M. Huntington Art Gallery, University of Texas at Austin, 1983).

Celebrating Generations
and Their Accomplishments

Roland G. Roessner, Jr., Elizabeth Danze, Evan K. Taniguchi, and Tommy Cowan

GENERATIONS OF STUDENTS have walked through the doors of the School of Architecture since its creation a century ago. Those students have found their lives entwined as parents, children, friends, colleagues, predecessors, and peers through The University of Texas at Austin. This collection of stories celebrates the architectural careers and accomplishments of fathers and the children who followed in their footsteps.

Roland G. Roessner, Jr.
(BArch '76), President, Sixthriver Architects

World War II changed the world as we knew it and propelled America in new directions. After serving in the United States Navy's civil engineering corps, my father, Roland G. Roessner, Sr., was recruited for a faculty position by the chairman of the Department of Architecture (which, at the time, was in the College of Engineering). During his career at UT (1948-1982), my father saw residential architecture flourish and pioneered programs that have forever changed our industry and the school itself.

My father was recognized as a mentor to students who espoused the idea that architecture was a practical science. His knowledge of professional practice, along with real-life experience, and his ability to communicate that practical experience to students was a great combination. Few architects tied their professional practice and their design studios so closely together. He was responsible for establishing the school's Professional Residency Program and was an early proponent of the use of computers to enhance teaching and architectural communication with clients. The Professional Residency Program, which continues to flourish today, provides students with on-the-job training within their profession before the completion of their degree and coursework.

As the only child of a practicing architect, I grew up listening to notable architects, artists, and educators, such as O'Neil Ford and my uncle, Palm Springs architect Roger Williams, debating the future of the industry. Architecture was a part of our family's everyday life, and I was fortunate to be surrounded by these influential, forward-thinking people while growing up. My father officed from home, and the architectural models from his projects became my playground. The unique scents of cigarette and cigar smoke, eraser dust, glue, sawdust, coffee, and iced tea were like the aroma of comfort food to me at a young age. The details, craftsmanship, and designs were spectacular without any reliance on technology-based design tools, such as computers and drafting programs—architects were forced to think in three dimensions through hand-drawn sketches.

It wasn't until I went to college that I realized my career path would in some ways parallel my father's. The very programs that my dad created at UT (in some cases, decades earlier) would be the catalyst for my career as well as the careers of many friends and colleagues. During my fifth year in the bachelor of architecture program, I toured a Houston firm with my father and my roommate, who was also an architecture student, as part of the Professional Residency Program. With fifteen hours of credit and a $1,500 scholarship, which was my stipend for seven months, I learned a tremendous amount about my field and had an epiphany that, while my passion for architecture was much like my father's, my path would be much different. Commercial architecture and interiors piqued my interest and would allow me, fresh out of school, to work on notable architectural projects in Houston and Washington D.C., such as the Transco Tower, the Sweetwater Country Club, the Harris County Astrodome, the headquarters for U.S. Airways, and the Social Security Administration.

Although our professional paths went in opposite directions, I did have the honor of working on several

Kozmetsky Residence, Austin, TX, 1977, prior to renovation and, above, revised design created 30 years later

projects with my father. Among these was the Kozmetsky Residence. In 1977, my father was asked to design this weekend retreat for his dear friends, Dr. George and Ronya Kozmetsky. I was honored to have my father ask me to assist him on this project, which won a Texas Society of Architecture Honor award. Thirty years after we created its design, I was surprised to be asked by the Kozmetsky's daughter, Nadia, to remodel the project. The house had been a joy to work on with my father and was so again decades later when I revised and updated it in his memory. It is a living testament to the love of a father and a son and the importance of trust from a great friend and client.

More than thirty years into my own career, I am incredibly humbled and proud of my father's legacy to architecture and his influence over me and the students he taught during his tenure at the School of Architecture. His legacy continues through all of us as graduates of the program.

Elizabeth Danze
(BArch '81), FAIA, Principal, Danze Blood Architects
Associate Professor, Distinguished Teaching Professor

At the end of August 1952, my father, Leo Danze (BArch '55), arrived by train at the downtown Austin station. He had come from New York City via Colorado, bringing with him a load of books, a suitcase of mostly winter clothes and a Naugahyde shaving kit that was a hand-me-down from a friend. He still has the kit today. He made his way to the UT campus and was immediately struck by the beauty of its buildings and the easy atmosphere that pervaded the grounds.

With his family and friends many miles away, he focused on his studies, working day and night at the School of Architecture, and, not having a watch of his own, he looked to the clock on the Tower as his timepiece. He made lifelong friends at the school, several of whom he still meets regularly today. After graduation, he went to work with a fellow classmate for an architect who primarily designed houses, which was the building type my father was most interested in. It was at this firm that he met H. Ross Davis, his future business partner, and, together, they built Danze & Davis Architects, which is celebrating its fiftieth anniversary this year.

It is a special experience to grow up with a parent who is an architect. My father always found his work interesting and challenging, and I was inspired by his unfailing enthusiasm for going to the office each day. He believed that a small house could be noble and that it was a worthwhile endeavor to design a home for the average family, not only for the well heeled. He believed that money was not necessarily a requirement for good design and that everyone should have a well designed, efficient, and affordable house. He found great joy and pleasure in the act of designing a building and knew that he could affect people's lives through that work.

Danze Blood Architects with Leo Danze, Darden Hill Ranch School, Driftwood, TX, 1995

He showed me how important it was to make a positive contribution in the world. Specifically, he showed me that the service architects provide extends far beyond satisfying our clients' direct needs. We, as architects, touch each person who occupies our buildings in some way. Even if it's only a small thing, it can have a powerful and meaningful effect. These guiding principles I learned from my father, and they profoundly inform and guide my own work as an architect and educator.

Evan K. Taniguchi
(attended UTSOA '72-'77), Principal, Taniguchi Architects

Looking back, there's not anything that single-handedly persuaded me to follow my father, Alan Y. Taniguchi, FAIA, into architecture, mainly because there's so much to consider, due to his success in both the profession and academia (and social activism throughout both careers). So, I would have to say that I naturally evolved into an architect (and social activist), since it literally surrounded me while I was growing up.

It all started when Alan and Leslie (I've always referred to them by their first names since we worked together in our "family" business for so long) moved to Harlingen, Texas (the Valley), in 1950 from the Bay Area, where Alan had graduated from the University of California, Berkeley, and worked for Anshen and Allen on their Eichler home projects. Upon arrival in the Valley, while opening a small practice, Alan also built the house that my brother and I grew up in. Of course, it was a modern Eichler-style home: exposed post-and-beam, flat roof, floor-to-ceiling glass, and transite (concrete board) siding. The interior was basically an open plan with a more private bedroom-wing appendage, cork floors, built-in storage with resin-coated-insect-screen sliding-door panels, built-in furnishings, Eames chairs, and cubist art. Aside from the natural finishes, the only color was a vivid orange, which complemented the cork. I remember our friends would go home and tell their parents that the Taniguchis lived in an unusual house, that it looked like a shoebox with a bunch of glass walls, and that the furniture was very uncomfortable. Ironically, the houses he designed in the Valley at that time are now collector items, similar to the Eichlers in California.

As kids, my brother and I always spent a lot of time (many sleepovers) at "the office," especially when there were project deadlines. Leslie would be up all night piecing together the specs and then printing them out on an old mimeograph machine. In-house blueprints consisted of exposing the print paper and vellum to direct sunlight and then putting it in a tube that had a rag soaked with ammonia in it (whew!). And, this being the 1950s, everyone smoked cigarettes. How anyone delivered a set of contract documents back then still amazes me.

Because Alan became so well known as a practitioner and dean of the School of Architecture (1968-1972), I was fortunate to meet many of his colleagues, who also inspired me—Louis Kahn, Buckminister Fuller, O'Neil Ford, to name a few. Since O'Neil and Alan were such good friends, our family spent quite a few weekends at the Fords' Willow Way compound in San Antonio. What I best remember are the peacocks, Alan trimming O'Neil's hair (Alan had been a barber in his internment camp during WWII), and O'Neil telling us about witnessing a decapitation and watching the head roll down the hill. And later on, when I wasn't interested in finishing college, I'd always remind Alan that O'Neil never received a college degree and was proud of it.

My most inspiring memory of Alan's deanship is the parties that my parents would throw for the students and faculty. Being the late 1960s, these parties somewhat resembled a small version of Woodstock, and a few were thrown on the riverboat that would cruise Town Lake (now Lady Bird Lake). The long-haired students (which meant all of the students) were always at the back of the boat, so the smoke of burning herbs would carry downstream (they were practicing what they learned about site orientation and prevailing breezes), and the faculty members would be carrying on and

dancing to the Beatles, Rolling Stones, Grateful Dead, Credence, etc. Many of the faculty were quite young (and hip) at that time—true characters such as Owen (and Judy) Cappleman, Richard Dodge, Sinclair Black, Gerlinde Leiding, Dick Oliver, Wolff Hilbertz, Pliny and Daria Fisk, and others. I loved those parties and the camaraderie that was so prevalent in the school back then. At the time, I was still in high school and would invite my innocent friends along. When their parents heard about these parties, I'm sure many discouraged their children from pursuing an architectural education. Like Woodstock, the School of Architecture will never experience anything like that again.

I've pretty much maintained the same principles and office culture in my current practice but, unfortunately, have been forced to focus on more business-related issues because of the fierce competition and short timelines for most projects. Without a marketing department (it's just me), we have been lucky to survive for so long, always picking up a design and/or planning project in the nick of time, many for the City of Austin and the University. The two most visible are the Palmer Events Center (Barnes Taniguchi Centerbrook) for the city and the Norman Hackerman Building (CO Architects+Taniguchi) for UT. It's very ironic that CO Architects was originally Anshen and Allen of Los Angeles, and that Alan began his career in their San Francisco office approximately sixty-two years ago. We've come the full circle, but I'm not done yet.

Of all those things that influenced me, I appreciate Alan's social consciousness the most. Whether he was diversifying the school with women and minorities, speaking out against the Vietnam War, supporting his

Taniguchi Architects, Van Erp Residence, Austin, TX AIA/Austin Award, 1982

Taniguchi
Architects, United
States Embassy
Building,
Georgetown,
Guyana. AIA/Austin
Award, 1992

And while the children of great architects have forged their own careers in this industry, the fathers certainly have their own memories of the past and are bursting with pride as they watch the next generation build the future.

Tommy Cowan
(BArch '68, MArch '70), FAIA, retired

Having two children with outstanding musical talent and no apparent interest in architecture as I was developing my practice, you can imagine my surprise when after a year in pre-law at UT, my son, Michael, announced that he would be transferring to the University of Texas at Arlington for architecture (possibly to escape mom and dad at home...). And, two years later, to have my daughter, Terri, announce that she would be going away to Iowa State on a Band Scholarship but would be enrolling in their Graphic Arts program (also far away from home).

While every father would sacrifice for his children, upon graduation, Michael and I agreed that we would not attempt to practice in the same firm, and that while I would be an advisor on call, I would not meddle in his career. Michael had been working in Dallas with Carter and Burgess when his wife was awarded a scholarship for a master's in child psychology at the University of Texas at San Antonio, and they relocated. Without my "advice." Michael selected Kell–Muñoz (KMW) to interview with and called the next week to announce that, without my help, he had been offered a job. While pleased with his initiative, I was disappointed that I did not have a chance to meddle.

students who were attempting to save the trees on Waller Creek, or helping preserve our Capitol view corridors, his intent was to make our world a better place. In fact, his most satisfying moment was when he received the AIA's Whitney Young Award at the National Convention in 1997, which recognized all of his efforts. When Alan passed away in 1998, I was asked to take over his seat on the Board of Trustees at Huston-Tillotson University, and I ended up serving ten years there. Aside from having a great deal of previous community activity, I currently serve on the boards of the Austin History Center Association and the National Japanese-American Museum, and lend my planning skills to the Austin Comprehensive Plan Task-Force. My goal, too, is to make this a better place.

Although my career would not have evolved to where it is without my father's overall influence, my mother played a huge role in it all and must be equally recognized. And special thanks to Fred Clarke (BArch '70, FAIA, Pelli Clarke Pelli), and his wife Laura, for recognizing Alan's contributions to the school, as well as to their own lives, by establishing a scholarship in his name. Alan would tell me the story about how Fred was hired by Cesar Pelli after a design studio jury before Fred had even graduated. Fred came back later to finish his degree and then became a partner in his firm. Alan received many prestigious awards during his career, but this recognition is the most inspirational to me, since it comes from a very successful professional who understands and appreciates what helped get him there.

Tommy and Michael Cowan, Graebar, Simmons & Cowan, Health Science Building, Texas A&M University, Round Rock, TX, 2009

Two weeks after Michael went to work, a face he had not seen during his interview (Henry Muñoz) appeared in his drafting bay and announced that the partners of the firm would like to speak with someone named "Cowan." Like being called to the principal's office, Michael feared dismissal. Henry asked why Michael had not disclosed his relationship to me during the interview and was relieved when Henry advised that I was a good friend and that he was happy to have him at KMW. Dads are not always a liability...

When Michael and his family returned to Austin seven years ago and started his firm—Haddon Cowan Architects Collaborative—we did find some common ground to practice on and have enjoyed several projects.

The most recent is the Health Science Building for Texas A & M University in Round Rock.

In closing: for more than a century, The University of Texas at Austin has served the architecture community as an educator, sounding board, and support network. As graduates of the School of Architecture and children of great architects who preceded us, the university has provided us with the foundation to build our careers, the tenacity to be great at what we do, and the humility to look back and appreciate what we've learned, created, and celebrated. It is with great honor that we share our stories, memorialize our fathers, and congratulate the School of Architecture on 100 years of excellence.

Change

Hal Box, W. L. Moody, Jr., Centennial Professor Emeritus; Former Dean, 1976-1992.

ONE WAY TO EXPLORE the future of the School of Architecture is by examining where we have been, considering the accelerating rate of change to the present, and extrapolating that rate of change to five, ten, and twenty years from now. Twenty years can appear far away, but because I have observed the school for sixty-four years as student, alumnus, dean, professor, and professor emeritus, it does not seem so long to me. I believe we can imagine such periods of time and set goals we can achieve.

Just consider what was happening here sixty-four years ago. The walls of the lobby and hallways of the Architecture Building (it didn't become Goldsmith Hall until 1978) were filled with beautiful, watercolor renderings of dazzling techniques. In 1946, there was no air conditioning—the windows were open in August. There was incandescent lighting, no fluorescents. Of course there were no computers, nor were there blueprint machines. History lectures were illustrated with black and white lantern slides. There were no guest lectures. There was no endowment. The tuition was $50 per semester. The building was closed at 10:00 p.m. every night; students were required to leave, or hide out, as we sometimes did to continue to work. The school was a department within the College of Engineering, and we had a chairman rather than a dean. The entire staff consisted of one secretary. There were over 600 students, not much smaller than our size today, but everyone was crammed into one building.

BOX | 29

Studio life was as vital as it is today, but with differences. All design projects were presented in watercolor drawn on a "stretch"—an expensive, heavy Whatman paper, usually 30" x 40"—that was soaked in water in a large basin in each studio, then glued on its edges to a drawing board and left to dry overnight, so that it would be tight as a drum to draw on the next day. Drawings were done with India ink held between two sharp steel nibs of a ruling pen, and watercolor applied with Russian sable-hair brushes. Final projects were "juried" by faculty in a closed room with no students present—the drawings had to speak for themselves—and judged in the Beaux-Arts manner with 1st Mention, 2nd Mention, 3rd Mention, X-D, and X-F. Only then were the students allowed to enter and to receive their "prizes."

In the no-man's land between the Ecole des Beaux-Arts and "Gropian Modernism," we started each new five-week studio project with an *esquisse*, a sketch problem for which we analyzed a given site, building type, and functions and came up with a *parti*, an architectural concept, in eight or twelve hours. From that point on, we were to refine the *parti* into a work of architecture, carefully considering composition, proportion, form, and mass. Today, it seems that we've swung from the absurdity of the old time allocation —one day for analysis and concept and twenty days for building design—to the opposite extreme of maybe 75 percent of studio time spent on analysis, followed by a frantic charette when the building is designed without the refinement of composition, proportion, mass, and form. I submit that we need to find a better balance.

In the late 1940s, the architecture library, then in what today is the large studio on the second floor of Goldsmith Hall, was a comfortable room with a small collection. All of the Beaux-Arts folios had been moved up high on the top shelves, and the lower shelves were filled with many Corbu and Wright monographs, some Aalto, along with Sigfried Giedion's *Space, Time and Architecture*, Lewis Mumford, CIAM publications, and a limited number of journals such as *Arts & Architecture*, *Pencil Points*, *Architectural Forum*, *Architectural Record*, and the *Engineering News Record*. We were consumed with what was new.

The architectural engineering program was in the same building and had the same courses through second-year design. This combination provided a head start to the engineers and grounded the architects in the realities of building. This valuable educational association was lost in the 1950s. The planning program met several blocks away on 26th Street.

Many of the veterans returning from World War II were interested in architecture. Three hundred freshmen architecture students met in Hogg Auditorium for Chairman Hugh McMath's first-year lecture course—the one that I later gave and that Larry Speck later made famous. Four students shared a studio desk in first-year design where our initial "basic" design project was to design a three-bedroom house. It was basic as a building, but there were no exercises in proportion or composition or what we call basic design today. Several semesters of freehand drawing and watercolor were required.

None of the faculty in 1946 actively practiced architecture. Educated under the influence of the Ecole des Beaux-Arts, they were newly aware of Modernism, trying to understand it, and leading us in the best way they could. We were confused. Harvard's Gropius told us to not look back, but he didn't tell us where to look. By the fall of 1948, Martin Kermacy and Roland Roessner arrived with better understandings of the new directions in architecture. I had the good fortune to work for O'Neil Ford in the summer of my third year, and for the rest of school worked half-time for Charles Granger who had apprenticed under Richard Neutra and Eero Saarinen.

In light of the crowded conditions and outmoded pedagogy, it is surprising that the graduates of 1949 to 1951 would go on to head some of the top firms in the state and some of the largest in the nation: Dahl, Braden and Jones; Marmon and Mok; Peters and Field; Sheffleman and Nix; Pratt and Box. Bill Brubaker became president of Perkins and Will, Vic Vickery in Chicago, Charles Lawrence became head of design for CRS, and Vic Neuhouse and Harwood Taylor founded 3DI International.

I made my career in Dallas and from a distance observed the educational innovations that Harwell Hamilton Harris inspired in the 1950s and the social activism of the 1960s that led to our specialized degree programs in historic preservation and sustainable design. One of the most significant events in the school's history occurred one morning in 1969 when the chairman of the Board of Regents, Frank Erwin, sought to cut down mature trees along Waller Creek to make room for the expansion of the stadium. Dozens of architecture students had climbed into the trees in protest. As the bulldozers came on the scene, Erwin ordered Dean Alan Taniguchi, the extraordinary architect, teacher, activist, and the planner of Town Lake (now Lady Bird Lake), to get the students out of the trees. Taniguchi refused. Standing toe-to-toe, the chairman is alleged to have said, "Architecture was on the top of the list for a new building here by the stadium, but you are at the bottom of the list now." Taniguchi said, "But we need more space for our growth." To which the chairman replied, "We will limit your enrollment; you won't grow." He made good on the threat, but the result was a great gift; we kept our Paul Cret building and limited our enrollment to the best students available, while other state schools had to accept unrestricted enrollment. That three-minute confrontation changed the course of the school, so that that we now have the best architecture on campus and the highest SAT scores among entering freshmen in the university.

In 1976, I was invited to Austin to be interviewed for the deanship, which had been in flux despite strong efforts by those who held the position in the years since Taniguchi's resignation. I was happy in Dallas with the school I had started at the University of Texas at Arlington, my firm, and my family and was not much interested in the job. But my former professor, Roland Roessner, insisted that I come talk. I agreed to meet with President Lorene Rogers and offer my assessment of the school's critical needs. I told her the Architecture Building needed renovation and expansion; the school needed all of Sutton Hall rather than the few rooms it was using, and that building, too, needed renovation; Battle Hall was needed for the architecture library; and the graduate program needed enhancement with new faculty.

The president asked for a copy of my notes, and I left thinking I had done what I came to do. It was a surprise when she called me later that afternoon to say that the university could meet all of my conditions and went on to ask what I wanted as a salary and when I could begin. I had inadvertently negotiated a really big deal that turned out to be $24 million in building construction. Not wanting the job, I asked for a huge salary, which was granted and brought a bit of respect to the school around campus. That fortunate outcome took ten times the three minutes of Taniguchi's confrontation, but it led to the physical facilities and equipment we have today.

Arriving in late August 1976, I was surprised that the dean didn't have an office and that faculty meetings required a sergeant-at-arms with a gavel to keep order. The shouting matches from a small segment of faculty lasted only a couple of weeks, but some members of the staff were almost as hostile – it took three days to get a letter out the door. We had a receptionist, a Dean's Assistant, two clerk-typists, a staff of two for Planning, a slide librarian with no storage equipment other than cardboard boxes in a small closet, and a shop master, Mike Farmer—a staff of seven compared to our current staff of around thirty. There was no endowment—travel expenses, research support, special events, were funded out of the faculty's own pockets. Social functions were funded out of the dean's pocket or by the Student Council. This was a time when, if I wanted to have an all-school meeting, I simply asked the president of the Student Council to buy a keg of beer and put it in the middle of the courtyard—the studios would empty instantly and everyone would assemble in the courtyard.

Setting goals and achieving them had been my way of making things happen in starting my firm in Dallas and the school in Arlington, but the dean's job in Austin was not new. It was hobbled by history, and I realized that I had to think beyond my tenure as dean to visualize what it would take for the school to excel. The good news was that the university administration was anxious to improve the school and responded to our needs, making good on all its promises for building improvements and construction.

At a meeting of the school's faculty in charge of leadership in Cuernavaca in the summer of 1987, we changed the emphasis of the school from the preparation for the practice of architecture to preparation for broader concerns of the discipline of architecture. The following year we organized a major goal-setting exercise to help us determine our path to excellence and formulate a convincing proposal to the university for support. The well funded Goals Conference, professionally organized and staffed, was attended by key people from the university and the architecture deans of Harvard, MIT, Cornell, Arizona State, the University of Oregon, and the University of Virginia. The group endorsed our plan to expand the school to include the disciplines of interior design and landscape architecture, to make historic preservation a degree program, and to develop doctoral

BOX | 31

programs. Deans Larry Speck and Fritz Steiner have accomplished these goals and more. I believe we should consider also adding a master of science program in development and, perhaps, a master of science degree in building construction or construction management.

Change has led us to be one of the top schools in the country, ranked with Harvard, Yale, Columbia, and MIT. We can plan for long-term growth in excellence. One hundred years is not so long—I've lived 80 percent of the school's life span. What do we do next?

The Texas Rangers Era

Having achieved administrative autonomy in 1950, the School of Architecture sought to redefine its pedagogical identity. Harwell Hamilton Harris, a prominent California architect known for his allegiance to a regionally inflected modernism, was appointed director in 1951 and proceeded to hire a diverse group of energetic, young faculty members whom he charged with restructuring the early years of the curriculum. In addition to Bernhard Hoesli, who had joined the faculty shortly before Harris's appointment, other new arrivals included Colin Rowe, John Hejduk, Robert Slutzky, and Lee Hirsche. They later became known as the Texas Rangers. Harris's ability to manage the school and win the support of the senior faculty fell short of his ambition, and he resigned his position in 1955. Most of the younger faculty left the university shortly thereafter, but those who stayed, including Richard Swallow and Eugene George, retained and refined aspects of the new pedagogy, and its influence can be found in the school today.

Alexander Caragonne recalls the student body then in his book, *The Texas Rangers: Notes from an Architectural Underground* (1995):

We, the class of 1958, were a typical sampling of the middle-class Texas subculture of the period. Along with small-town greenhorns like myself...there were older students, too: Avery Bowen, ex-military police and Korean War veteran, and ex-Navy man George Englert. There was, I recall, one young woman, Mary Dring...and two Hispanics, Louis Viramontes and Jerry Vineigra. There was one black student, Ira Lott; but for the most part my classmates were all young, white males from the urban areas of the state: Dallas, Houston, Austin, and San Antonio.

Well, what happened was a group of people came down and met. A handful of people without any pre-plan. In a funny way, it was just the chemistry of the individuals, which is so unpredictable. There was no pre-planning...we just happened!

–John Hejduk

Left: Colin Rowe working with a student in a design class

Below: Buckminster Fuller, seen with Leipziger-Pearce and Harris, visited the school in February 1954

After his resignation, Harris commented on the challenges of his tenure as Director of the school. He emphasized administrative duties, the restrictive low budget, and the difficulty of inheriting "a solid core of incompetents protected by tenure."

School of Architecture Faculty, 1954-1955, from left to right: Hugh McMath, Lee Hirsche, Joseph Buffler, Goldwin Goldsmith, Hugo Leipziger-Pearce, John Hejduk, Harwell Hamilton Harris, Roland Gommel Roessner, Robert Slutzky, Colin Rowe, Bernhard Hoesli, Martin Kermacy, Kenneth Nuhn, Robert White

The Texas Rangers' approach to design focused on manipulating spatial properties by using historical precedents and Gestalt principles. The first-year design studio included composition exercises like those originated at the German Bauhaus in the 1920s. Students worked with basic elements of design—dot, line, plane, form— before considering architectural and programmatic applications. Line drawings helped students discern "negative space," and they investigated the physiological effects of color perception. Historical and contemporary buildings were studied to help explore spatial ideas. The diverse faculty and visiting lecturers, including Louis Kahn in 1952-1953, exposed the students to various professional approaches.

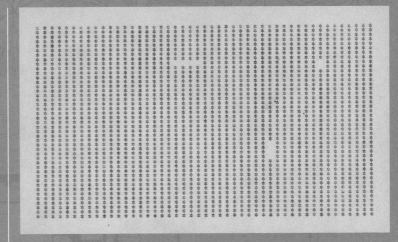

W. Bryan Thruston (BArch '57), An Interrupted Pattern Study: Junior Year, Robert Slutzky, Irving Rubin, and Lee Hirsche, critics, 1955

Frank Lloyd Wright with Harris and UT students at the Eighth Pan American Conference of Architects in Mexico City, 1952

Above: Architecture students boarding a train for a class trip to Chicago, 1954

Right: The Pace Setter House received local and national press. *The Dallas Times Herald* featured a special section on the project, October 10, 1954.

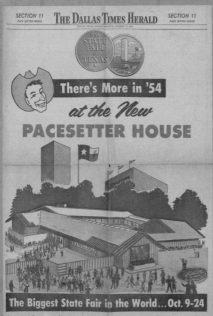

SECTION 11
PACE SETTER HOUSE

THE DALLAS TIMES HERALD

SECTION 11
PACE SETTER HOUSE

STATE FAIR TEXAS

There's More in '54
at the New
PACESETTER HOUSE

The Biggest State Fair in the World...Oct. 9-24

The Pace Setter House project allowed Harris to combine teaching and hands-on architectural practice. Designed for *House Beautiful* on the grounds of the 1954 Texas State Fair, the three-bedroom, all-electric house represented the latest in domestic modernism. Harris directed the work of six architecture students who prepared drawings and scale models for the project. The house was extensively photographed and published and visited by over 80,000 fair-goers.

Harris led trips to Mexico City, Chicago and St. Louis for fourth- and fifth-year architecture students. Such efforts introduced the students to the professional practice beyond their studies.

Theory and Practice

Lawrence W. Speck, W.L. Moody, Jr., Centennial Professor in Architecture; Distinguished Teaching Professor; Former Dean, School of Architecture, 1992-2001. Faculty member since 1975.

ONE OF THE GREATEST strengths of the School of Architecture that has contributed to its progress and stature over the last six decades (60 percent of its life) has been a special relationship between theory and practice that was established shortly after the school was separated from the College of Engineering in 1950. In the years immediately following that rebirth of architectural study at the University of Texas, an outstanding group of faculty members, often referred to as the Texas Rangers, descended on Austin and formulated a direction for architectural education that was fundamentally innovative and was the result of a unique collaboration and confluence of ideas.

When these individuals dispersed in the late 1950s, they took their diverse individual perspectives with them to many other distinguished schools of architecture around the globe and made significant contributions. But the confluence of their ideas—some notions about the bridging of theory and practice—remained here. It lay dormant for a period of time but emerged strongly again in the late 1970s and has continued to feed the school's fundamental growth since then.

Alexander Caragonne, in his book, *The Texas Rangers: Notes from an Architectural Underground*, outlines the story of this seminal period in the school's history, from 1951 to 1958, extraordinarily well.[1] Harwell Hamilton Harris was named director of the school just a year after it achieved its independent status. He came with a significant international reputation as a practitioner, but with no prior experience in academia. Thoughtful and well connected to progressive ideas in architecture through California colleagues like Richard Neutra and R. M. Schindler, Harris was reflective as well as pragmatic in his view toward architecture and architectural education. Caragonne notes that, "he was an architect, first, last, and always. He was a dedicated, pragmatic regionalist with a characteristic distrust of ideology and intellectualism."[2]

Bernhard Hoesli, a twenty-seven-year-old Swiss architect, had been recruited by the prior administration to join the faculty at the same time as Harris. In his mature career he would become one of the most renowned architectural educators in Europe, based at the ETH in Zurich. As Caragonne notes, Hoesli brought to UT, "a strong intellectual and methodological bias tempered with the pragmatic attitude of the practitioner."[3]

Colin Rowe was recruited by Harris to join the faculty in January of 1954. At thirty-three, this brilliant British intellectual was already an accomplished architectural critic. He would go on to become one of the great American architectural educators of his era from his home base at Cornell University. (In 1985 he was awarded the Topaz Medallion, the highest honor given in architectural education in North America, presented to only one individual each year.) Caragonne notes that at Texas, Rowe "imparted to his students a level of scholarship and theory exceptional in the design studios of the period."[4]

According to Rowe, he and Hoesli joined forces early on with two tenured faculty members, Hugo Leipziger-Pearce and Martin S. Kermacy, to become a sort of "palace guard" in opposition to the entrenched old-timers who resisted the changes that were afoot.[5] Leipziger-Pearce, who was forty-eight at the time, had studied at the Bauhaus in the era of Mies van der Rohe's directorship. Well versed in both the social and formal philosophy of modern architecture, his interests focused on community and regional planning. Kermacy at thirty-six was, as Caragonne notes, a "bona fide intellectual and scholar."[6] He had been trained at the University of Pennsylvania where he developed a strong interest in twentieth-century architectural history as well as in design.

Twelve additional faculty members, whom Caragonne categorizes as "reformers," were added in the era 1954

to 1958. They were either recruited by Harris, Hoesli, or Rowe, or aligned themselves with the new program soon after they arrived. John Hejduk, for example, had worked in the same office as Hoesli in New York and was attracted to Austin by Hoesli's description of an opportunity to work in a place where independent thought was possible under enlightened leadership. (Hejduk won the Topaz Medallion in 1988 after many years leading the architecture program at Cooper Union.)

Bob Slutzky and Lee Hirsche had been students of Josef Albers at Yale, where Harris had been a visiting critic shortly before coming to Austin. Rowe had also studied at Yale from 1951 to 1952 under Henry Russell Hitchcock and suggested that Albers' students teach freshman drawing classes in the new curriculum at UT.

Blake Alexander (BArch '50), who had gone on for graduate study at Columbia University after completing his professional degree here, and Lee Hodgden, who had worked for both O'Neil Ford and Alvar Aalto, were other Harris appointees who quickly took up the cause. John Shaw (BArch '50), a recent UT graduate, and Werner Seligmann, who was initially assigned to teach working drawings, had been recruited by the old guard but almost immediately aligned themselves with the other younger faculty after they arrived. (Seligmann won the Topaz Medallion in 1998 after a long career teaching at Cornell and Syracuse University.)

Jon Bowman, who was hired to teach structures, and Richard Swallow, who, along with Hodgden, helped organize the outline for first-year design courses, arrived late enough in the game that it was natural for them to get thoroughly swept up in the emerging curricular and teaching innovations. Eugene George (BArch '49) also came later in the era and had a similar influential role in the sophomore curriculum as Swallow had in the freshman curriculum.

By 1958, as Caragonne describes in salacious detail, personal and petty bickering brought the Texas Rangers program to a disappointing end. Harris left abruptly in 1955. Rowe, Hejduk, Slutzky, and Hirsche left in 1956. Hoesli left in 1957 and Shaw, Hodgden, and Seligmann followed in 1958. Notably, Leipziger-Pearce, Kermacy, Alexander, George, Bowman, and Swallow stayed at Texas.

The eighteen or so individuals who participated in the Texas Rangers program held widely disparate views of architecture, as their subsequent careers attest. Perhaps their only substantial common ground was their desire for reformation of architectural education and their commitment to being excellent teachers. Even when Rowe, Hodgden, Shaw, and Seligmann were teaching together at Cornell in the 1960s, Rowe was clearly at odds with his former Texas colleagues. Among those who practiced architecture in subsequent years, the warm, tactile work of Harris after he left Texas could hardly be more different from the boxy, white modernism of Seligmann or the sometimes voluptuous, fanciful, and colorful work of Hejduk.

In terms of their perspectives on theory and practice, the divergence between these individuals is striking as well. Colin Rowe would become the godfather of a movement toward abstract and highly intellectual architectural theory as a generator for architectural design in the 1980s, while Harwell Harris would write in 1986, "Architecture may express ideas, but it is not made of ideas. Ideologies are for the creator to avoid."[7] Bernard Hoesli would land somewhere in between and would influence a generation of architects at ETH, including Jacques Herzog, Pierre de Meuron, and Santiago Calatrava, who would find a reciprocal relationship between theory and practice.

I would argue that what moved away from UT in the diaspora of the late 1950s was the many divergent perspectives of the individuals who contributed to the Texas Rangers. What stayed was the rich merging of their ideas that had occurred in the short period of the mid-1950s. Though they took some time to germinate, the seeds planted by the Texas Rangers have had a lasting effect on the approach to architectural education in the School of Architecture.

By the time I came to UT in 1975, all seventeen faculty members Caragonne describes as the "old guard" in his saga were gone. Five of the opposition—Alexander, Kermacy, Bowman, Swallow and Leipziger-Pearce—had become the senior faculty of the school. The defeated rebels were the new power structure. The five of us who were recruited in tenure-track positions that fall—Michael Benedikt, Michael Garrison, Larry Doll, Ivan Zaknic and myself—were about as divergent in our perspectives as the motley crew that Harris collected.

Benedikt was an erudite and intellectual South African who had done his post-professional work at Yale.

Garrison was a nuts-and-bolts pragmatist who got his graduate degree from Rice and was interested, well ahead of his time, in what is now called sustainability. Doll had done his graduate work at Cornell under the tutelage of some of the Texas Rangers and was interested in methodology in general and morphology in particular. Zaknic was a political refugee from Yugoslavia who had spent time in Paris and New York and was a dedicated Corbusian. I had done all three of my degrees at M.I.T. and was committed to becoming an active practitioner.

The same kind of diverse accumulation of a range of people with balanced interests in both theory and practice that Alexander, Kermacy, Bowman, Swallow and Leipziger-Pearce had witnessed in the Texas Rangers days was replicated in the era when they were finally in positions of power. In the 1975 casting for the re-enactment, Benedikt might have been selected to play the role of Colin Rowe—the consummate theorist. I might have been cast as the Harwell Harris character—an architect "first, last and always" and a dedicated pragmatist. Doll, Garrison, and Zaknic might have played the more nuanced roles of Slutzky, Seligmann and Hoesli.

Pedagogically, what happened in the decades that followed was not so different from what happened in the Texas Rangers era. A succession of diverse groups of young faculty was put in charge of re-working the curriculum and teaching the key courses in it. Socially and politically, however, the era that began in the late 1970s was nothing like the 1950s. When the remnants of the Texas Rangers got to be senior faculty, they behaved very differently than the old guard of their early years. Alexander, Kermacy, Bowman, Swallow, and Leipziger-Pearce were all extremely supportive of their younger colleagues and continually promoted a progressive spirit of change in the school.

When Hal Box became dean in 1976, he helped establish a period of pluralism and respect for diverse perspectives. Theory and practice became not only balanced in the school, but, progressively, the border between them became more and more blurred. Through the 1980s and 1990s, as many of the best schools of architecture became very theory heavy, UT resisted a tilt to that extreme. As many other programs reacted with a bias toward pragmatism and technology in the first decade of the 21st century, UT resisted that bias as well.

In fact, there came to be a preference at UT for a very soft boundary between theory and practice. Faculty members who write extensively on architectural theory, such as Michael Benedikt and Steven Moore, teach design studios often with a very strong practical focus. Faculty members generally thought of as practitioners and who have a longstanding track record of building, like David Heymann and me, are teaching core theory classes for graduate students. Exclusive sub-disciplinary categorizations in this arena have been broken down by the shared conviction that both the intellectual and the practical sides of architecture will benefit from a diminution of boundaries between them.

There is, in fact, a long tradition of theoretical positions in architecture emerging from very pragmatic roots—all the way back to Vitruvius and Alberti. Steven Moore, for example, has been extending that tradition at UT for many years by taking very practical notions of resource distribution and conservation and using them as a springboard for theoretical and political positions about justice and social equity.

Likewise, there is a long record of very practical problems in architecture being resolved most cogently by designers who have strong theoretical positions. Kahn's well articulated notions about order or Aalto's clearly stated advocacy for function helped them create very practical plans that resolved real challenges of building use. Exeter Library or the Kimbell Museum by Kahn as well as Baker House or Paimio Sanatorium by Aalto are very practical buildings that resolve complicated programmatic problems through powerful theoretical ideas.

This kind of practical use of theory to solve architectural problems is firmly rooted in the design work of faculty members like David Heymann whose theoretical ideas about nature and landscape help him create architecturally significant solutions to pragmatic problems of site drainage and storm-water disposal. It is clearly evident in projects by Juan Miró where he applies his convictions about the expressive nature of structure and materials to solve fundamental problems of spanning or creating shelter. This kind of utilization of theory to solve practical problems is equally evident in the practice work of Kevin Alter and Ernesto Cragnolino, Elizabeth Danze and John Blood, Louise Harpman, Francisco Gomes, and Vince Snyder.

1 oct 05   La Tourette

Larry Doll, Ink drawing made at La Tourette, 1 October 2005

I am frequently impressed by the breadth of my colleagues in the realm of theory and practice. Their ability, as individuals, to merge the world of intellect and ideas with the world of practicality and building is inspiring. Anthony Alofsin, who is one of the most prolific thinkers/ writers on the faculty, took his architectural registration exam in his late fifties and is taking great pleasure in the practice of architecture. It is a natural extension of his more academic work. Wilfried Wang, another impressive intellect who is internationally known an author and critic is also conscientiously committed to the making of architecture with his practice partner, Barbara Hoidn.

There is a poignant essence of architecture that comes, not so much at the intersection of theory and practice, but at their true confluence. Perhaps this is one potential feature that is unique about architecture and that sets it apart from art or engineering. There is a particular magic that architecture creates when it truly merges the world of ideas with the pragmatic world of building and human inhabitation.

To bring the argument full circle, it was actually that merger of pragmatics and ideas that was fundamentally innovative in the pedagogy of the Texas Rangers in the 1950s. It was not just the strength of committed theorists like Colin Rowe or the enlightened building prowess of pragmatists like Harwell Harris that gave that era distinction. It was the confluence of the two, perhaps most evident in the exciting pedagogical work of Bernhard Hoesli.

That confluence is stronger than ever today in the School of Architecture and is a distinguishing feature of its programs. As I have visited and gotten to know architecture programs at dozens of schools in the United States and abroad, I have been impressed at how rarely this characteristic is evident in other programs. It is, indeed, a defining feature at the University of Texas that has deep roots and pervasive scope.

[1] Alexander Caragonne, *The Texas Rangers: Notes from an Architectural Underground* (Cambridge, MA: MIT Press, 1995).

[2] Ibid., p. 53.

[3] Ibid., p. 7.

[4] Ibid., p. 8.

[5] Ibid., p. 32

[6] Ibid., p. 16.

[7] Personal communication from Harwell Harris to David Thurmon, 24 September, 1986.

My Thirty-Five Years at
the School of Architecture

Michael Benedikt, Hal Box Chair in Urbanism; Director, Center for American Architecture and Design; ACSA Distinguished Professor. Faculty member since 1975.

I HAVE SPENT more than half my life teaching architecture at the University of Texas at Austin, and those thirty-five years comprise over a third of the school's history. Tell me it's not so!

I arrived in Austin from New Haven, Connecticut, in August of 1975, stepping out of the airport into a 100-degree afternoon and thinking, "Oh my God, what have I done?" Then-dean Chuck Burnette hired me, as well as Larry Speck, Larry Doll, Michael Garrison, and Ivan Zaknic (now at Lehigh University), in one fell swoop. Chuck was a visionary, clearly! Little did we know that he was in deep trouble with his faculty. He resigned a year later.

In thirty-five years, some things have not changed for me or for the school: the need to better incorporate the content of history and construction courses into/with studio; the eternal need for students to draw better; the musical-chairs dance of fitting teachers to curricula when many members of the faculty have important things to do besides teach; the stress of getting tenure and the zero-G behavior that follows it; the pride of seeing talented students do design work that is as good as any heralded architect (OK, they don't have the headaches of construction or budgets or real clients, so it's easier); but, perhaps above all, the excitement of feeling oneself to be a creative part of the evolution of architecture as a discipline—not just the experimenting, questioning, inventing part of the discipline, but the part that articulates and transmits architecture's oldest tricks, noblest moments, and most abiding values to succeeding generations.

People who have followed my writing over the years will sometimes remark at its diversity. True, it has undergone passages, from geeky studies of "isovists" and spatial perception to philosophizing about postmodernism and "reality" (*For an Architecture of Reality*, 1987), deconstructivism and meaning (*Deconstructing the Kimbell*, 1991), digital design and virtuality (*Cyberspace: First Steps*, 1991), economics and value (many papers), and evolution and theology (three new books). But for me they are all-of-a-piece, an unfolding of a handful of insights, from long ago, that marvelous architecture is marvelous for reasons yet to be fathomed, and that reality both is, and is not, exactly what it seems to be: solid and real, yet also a massive and sustained product of pure information flows, like the surface of an ocean. I continue to explore how architecture, from conception to execution to inhabitation, enfolds life and promotes it. And I remain convinced that "architectural thinking" is a unique mode of thought quite unlike that employed by writers, movie directors, scientists, chefs, painters, sculptors, composers, builders, or engineers, to name a few candidates for comparison: one can "think like an architect," to borrow the title of Hal Box's recent book (2007), about more things than buildings.

My teaching has followed the same path, especially in the seminar format where I consciously teach to my evolving interests. In studio, by contrast, I feel duty-bound to teach core competencies as well as to help students "be all they can be," although, inevitably, I cannot help but transmit certain enthusiasms and formal biases. Since teaching studio occupies most of my teaching time and is the core of architecture teaching at the school, permit me two sets of "over-the-years" observations:

1) As you know, architectural design is prone to falling into fashion eras, and I have seen my share come and go: modernism simpliciter, energy/sustainability (version 1.0), postmodernism, deconstructivism, neomodernism, digital and parametric design, biomimicry, energy/ sustainability (version 2.0), architecture as landscape... More interesting, perhaps, are the eternally recurring clashes between a limited number of more fundamental, often tacitly-held, preferences: the systems view vs. the experiential view, the control view vs. the open

view (of function), the primacy of physical construction (architecture = art of construction) vs. the primacy of social construction (architecture = art of community building) vs. the primacy of formal composition (architecture = art of "space making"), more recently digital vs. manual media in design, and running through all of these: elitism vs. populism, and the value of simplicity vs. the value of complexity. These conflicts show no sign of going away.

2) Some students imagine that the context of their work is the built environment—that what they design should be critiqued as propositions about how it would be, in the world, if their designs were built. Others figure out that the context of their work is actually architecture school, which is a different matter entirely, calling for different kinds of performance and a cannier understanding of frames of reference. Ironically, although the latter takes us further from simple, built reality, it may be closer to the reality of how success in life, as well as in architectural practice, is achieved. Likewise, it seems to me, there are teachers who nurture the first perspective, attracted to its idealism and sincerity, and those who nurture the second, attracted—in resignation or joy—to its realism. These two perspectives vie with each other still, and probably always will.

Let me turn finally to school governance and leadership. I have been privileged to serve four deans: Chuck Burnette, Hal Box, Larry Speck, and Fritz Steiner, remarkable men, all, whose faces were necessarily turned outward—towards the university, the community, the profession, and benefactors—as much as turned inward—toward teaching, hiring, budgeting, planning, and managing/leading/nursing "creatives." (Talk about herding cats!) The tireless efforts of all four to enhance the overall quality of the school while instituting ever-higher standards of justice and fairness have been a constant source of admiration to me and only occasional disappointment and frustration.

Certainly, all four of these leaders allowed me to make the contributions I could. In addition to the many, many committees I have chaired or served on, I have served as the Director of the Center for American Architecture and Design, following Larry Speck and Anthony Alofsin. The Center was the brainchild of Hal Box in 1985 at a moment of extreme optimism about the cultural role of architecture and a time of fervent and successful fundraising for the school and its then-new addition to

Goldsmith Hall. The Center has remained a singular venue for stimulating intellectual debate at the school, hosting national and international symposia on larger themes, and editing and publishing several book series: the award-winning *CENTER*, the smaller series CenterLine, and with the O'Neil Ford Professorship, the O'NF Monographs and Duographs.

I am proud to continue to serve as the Center's director; I am proud to hold the Hal Box Chair in Urbanism; I am proud to exchange ideas with the hardest-working and most talented group of faculty and staff any school of architecture could ask for. Above all, however, I am humbled that fate, thirty-five years ago, should have seen fit to place me at the University of Texas at Austin. I am a lucky man, at a jewel of a school, under a big Texas sky.

Student Activities

PTAH AND SPHINX CLUB

Now largely forgotten, the legend of Ptah passed through generations of UTSOA students. Ptah was the mascot of the Sphinx Club, an all-male architecture honor society founded in 1930. Sphinx initiates were well-known on campus for their mandatory orations from the balcony of Goldsmith Hall overlooking the West Mall. Passersby who failed to heed their architectural proclamations were pummeled with flour and water. Sphinx members chose Ptah-Nu as their figurehead because in Egyptian mythology Ptah is the god of creation and the patron of craftsmen and Nu is linked with the primary elements of earth and water, underscoring Ptah's mastery. Ptah's popularity grew beyond the Sphinx Club as architecture students and faculty donned Egyptian loincloths and bronzed their skin to portray Ptah and his loyal servants at the annual Wind-Up and Beaux-Arts balls. The tradition faded in the 1970s and 1980s, and Ptah's effigy is packed away in the Alexander Architectural Archive. Students today work unaware of the ancient Egyptian spirit watching over their studios.

WIND-UP AND BEAUX ARTS BALLS

UTSOA students and faculty have a long tradition of celebrating the end of the school year. The earliest parties were appropriately called Wind-Up Balls. The purpose remained the same, but the name was changed to the Beaux-Arts Ball in the 1950s. Early balls were held at the Driskill Hotel and included an appearance from Ptah, an awards ceremony, and the announcement of the Architecture Sweetheart. Faculty, students, and alumni were involved in creating costumes and decorations and planning the event. The tradition of the Beaux-Arts Ball continues with themes, rituals, and settings changing with the times.

Left: Sphinx Club initiates sounding off on the balcony of Goldsmith Hall (then Architecture Building), 1968

Below: Sphinx Club ceremony in the West Mall in front of the Goldsmith Hall, 1964

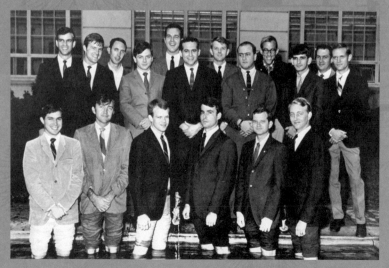

Sphinx Club members in the Goldsmith Hall courtyard, 1968

Ptah and Sphinx Club plaque, 1986

Students pay homage to their architectural heritage at a Wind-Up Ball

Left: Beaux-Arts Ball, An Explosion of the Senses, 2010

Top Right: Wind-Up Ball, 1938

Bottom Right: Exotic dancers entertain at the Beaux-Arts Ball, 1980

Social Activism

Beyond its unusual work habits and creative ways of letting off steam, the UTSOA community is well known for collective and individual activism on campus and beyond. Faculty have regularly taught courses based on interaction with governmental and non-profit organizations since the late 1930s, student organizations have a long history of mobilizing for volunteer efforts, and faculty and students alike have a record of personal activism in politics and public service.

The Alley Flat Initiative is one current example of the school's formal service-learning projects. Begun in 2005 as a joint effort of the Center for Sustainable Development, the Guadalupe Neighborhood Development Corporation, and the Austin Community Design and Development Center, the program develops prototypes for affordable, sustainable houses to be built along Austin's underutilized network of alleyways. Students have designed and participated in the construction of two homes to date.

Right: Students set up building blocks on the Main Mall as an outlet for self-expression and freedom of speech, 1971

Below: Students working on the second Alley Flat prototype, Lydia Street, 2009

As might be expected, faculty and students monitor developments on campus closely. At mid-century, students took their concerns regarding the quality of new campus buildings to the press. In a letter that caused a stir in the *Dallas Morning News* in 1949, they protested the new buildings Mark Lemmon had designed in the style of Paul Cret and argued, "If the university is to fulfill its role in developing the cultural background of the coming generation its entire attitude should be creative, not imitative." These words might have been used verbatim fifty years later in the controversy over the design of the Blanton Museum that led to the resignation of the original architects, Herzog & de Meuron Arkitekten, and Dean Larry Speck.

Faculty and students have also rallied on behalf of the historic buildings and landscapes. In 1989, Dean Hal Box, Professor Blake Alexander, and student action committees fought to save Anna Hiss Gymnasium from the wrecking ball. Their efforts helped convince the university to limit the destruction to the natatorium wing.

A protest that has acquired the patina of legend is the Battle of Waller Creek on October 22, 1969, when architecture students played a prominent role in resisting the university's effort to remove trees along Waller Creek to make room for the enlargement of the football stadium. In the face of bulldozers and the no less menacing countenance of Frank Erwin, the chairman of the Board of Regents, students held their ground, and Dean Alan Taniguchi refused the chairman's order to intervene in the standoff. Erwin had the protestors arrested and the trees cut down, but other students dragged branches up the hill and piled them in the entrance of Main Building. Some time later, architecture students organized a campaign to replant trees along the creek.

Left: Student occupying the remnants of a tree on Waller Creek, 1969

Right: Tree branches piled at the entrance to Main Building following the Battle of Waller Creek, 1969

Information Is Power . . .
If You Know Where to Find It

Martha González Palacios, Librarian, Architecture and Planning Library since 2008.

IN THE JANUARY 2010 issue of *Architect*, Robert A.M. Stern was interviewed regarding his firm's library. "You go to school for a long time, and then you go into an office, and you're often cut off from stimulation," he said of the start of his firm's collection of about 11,000 architectural tomes. "A good office library can be an indispensable resource for designers," the article continues. Stern sees the library as "the gateway to [their] architecture, conceptually. [They] do a lot of research—from both the aesthetic and technical points of view—in designing [their] buildings.'" His words reinforce both my experience as a former practicing architect and my opinion as an architecture librarian.

For the Architecture and Planning Library, the School of Architecture has been both its *raison d'être* and its closest ally. Programs at the school, many highly ranked, are supported by the library. Like the school, the library is considered among the top architecture and planning libraries in the country and is part of one of the largest research library systems in North America. With strong collections and services, a unique location, and a long history, the library has always been an integral part of the educational experience at the school.

The origins of the Architecture and Planning Library go back to a "seminar library" created in 1912 to support the newly established School of Architecture. There is little information about this modest, slow-growing collection and staff during its first decade, but thanks to the

Architecture Library in B. Hall, 1927

efforts of Hugo F. Kuehne, the School of Architecture's first faculty member, funds were secured to start the collection with an initial appropriation of $500.

It was not until October 1925, just prior to the first master of science degree offering, that the position of architecture librarian was created and assumed by Ruth H. Junkin who remained in this position for twenty years until she retired in 1945 at the age of seventy-two. During this time, she also apparently acted as unofficial advisor to the female architecture students. In her first annual report, dated February 24, 1926, she states that the collection had 954 volumes, and it is clear that up until then, the collection had not been formally organized or managed.

Throughout its history, the library has been housed in various buildings across campus. From the old Engineering Building (known today as the Gebauer

Building), the library moved with the school to its quarters in B. Hall (demolished in 1952), and to the new Architecture Building (Goldsmith Hall) in 1933. Subsequently, in 1973, as a result of the efforts of the school spearheaded by Dean Charles Burnette, the library moved to its present location at Battle Hall.

When three years later, the General Libraries (now known as the University of Texas Libraries) administration was considering moving the architecture collection to the nearly completed main branch—the Perry-Castañeda Library—the school, once again, successfully advocated for it to remain in Battle Hall. In a letter dated January 8, 1976 to the General Libraries director, Merle N. Boylan, Dean Burnette explained that "a fully dedicated and autonomous professional library close to studio spaces" was required since "architects use library resources somewhat differently than do other disciplines. Browsing

Left: Caricature of Ruth Junkin, architecture librarian from 1925 to 1945, stenciled on ceiling of the former Goldsmith Hall library

Right: Architecture Library, Goldsmith Hall, 1933

and quick reference are particularly important means of inspiration, verification, and technical decision-making during the direct, problem-solving activity that dominates architectural education." He further added, "no professional school which depends so heavily on case histories, visual information and both current and historic reference material can be very effective without its principal resource close at hand." Burnette's statements still ring true and are echoed in Stern's words thirty-four years later. Architecture and planning literature continues to be produced primarily on paper, so physical proximity is still extremely important for convenient browsing. Library circulation statistics show nearly 20 percent of material is used in the library but not formally checked out. Virtual proximity is also considered by striving to make electronic resources and services easily accessible.

In addition to its proximity, Battle Hall is a fitting home for an architecture library, given its architectural quality and historical significance. Battle Hall is one of two buildings on campus (the second one is Sutton Hall, also occupied by the School of Architecture) by prominent New York architect Cass Gilbert who, while serving as University Architect, designed Battle Hall to be the first library building for the university. It remained so until the Main Building's completion in 1937. Paul P. Cret's master campus plan from 1933 used Battle Hall's character-defining features and materials to set the tone for future construction on campus. Cret's plan, in turn, deeply influenced César Pelli & Associates' campus master plan from 1999, as seen in one of its major principles: "To use the architectural language of Paul Cret's original works as the point of departure for the design of new structures."

While the main purpose of the library is to support the curulular needs of the School of Architecture, the mission of the UT Libraries advances the academic mission of the university and enriches the intellectual life of the people of Texas by fostering information discovery, enabling teaching and research, nurturing creativity, partnering in the development and dissemination of new knowledge, and contributing to the intellectual growth and fulfillment of the individual.

In order to fulfill its mission, the library also serves the academic and research needs of scholars in affiliated disciplines and is an important resource for architecture and planning professionals. In turn, students, faculty, and staff from the school have access to well developed and unique collections that are far beyond the normal scope of an architecture and planning library at other UT libraries and research centers.

The Library and Collections Committee is active as a bridge between the school and the library by giving the library voice and providing invaluable insight into curricular developments. As times change, the committee is instrumental in keeping the library on track by meeting the changing needs and expectations of users. Work continues as the school and library adopt new technologies, collaborate, and provide more seamless integration of library services with instruction, both in classrooms and studios. Furthermore, to keep pace, the library must be involved from the very beginning when new programs or specialties are being considered. Collection assessment can be incorporated to the process to ensure that these new areas will be properly supported.

The library's physical and digital collections continue to grow: today the print collection is rapidly approaching

100,000 volumes, of which nearly 20,000 are part of Special Collections; the library has over 300 current subscriptions to magazines and journals and, as part of UT Libraries, licenses to hundreds of databases that ensure the discovery of articles and conference proceedings. The library also includes an architectural archive, a growing collection in the UT Digital Repository, and access from the catalogue to many free online publications.

On the other hand, the wealth of information found in the library and on the World Wide Web is irrelevant unless users have the skills to find what they need. The library plays a critical role in educating and enabling its users to tap into resources such as the first edition of Palladio's four books on architecture, *I Quattro libri dell'architettura* (1570), to books, articles, and images on the 2010 Pritzker laureates, SANAA. By further integrating library/research instruction with the curricula of the school, students and faculty can become not just information literate but information fluid, able to research effectively and efficiently. Instead of spending time trying to find information, they can focus on critical thinking, analyzing, evaluating, and creating.

The digital world has brought with it amazing possibilities to extend access and expand the range of ways to communicate. Information has become more ubiquitous, unruly, and unstable. As libraries embrace this new digital era they also take on the inherent challenges of organizing, presenting, and preserving electronic resources in meaningful ways for library users. Collecting and providing access to information is a main objective of libraries; unfortunately, most producers of digital resources are not concerned with long-term preservation and access. Until recently, preservation at a library meant the care of print material, which even if deteriorated, would remain usable, but digital media is much less stable and ownership can take many forms in the digital realm.

In order for the library collection to be well rounded, ongoing efforts persist to ensure the continued preservation and acquisition of print and digital materials, including retrospective collection development and the integration of electronic publications and resources that don't necessarily emulate their print predecessors. As in architecture, the learning curve for new technologies can be steep, but the potential benefits cannot be ignored.

The school's programs recognize the value of preservation, sustainability, technology, and innovative thinking; they know that these are not mutually exclusive, and the library shares this philosophy. Both in the virtual and physical realms, the library is very much alive, proud of its past and looking forward to its future as it continues to be one of the core resources for the School of Architecture, the University of Texas at Austin, and the architecture and planning community at large.

The Alexander Architectural Archive:
Value in the Sum of Its Parts

Beth Dodd, Head Librarian, Architecture and Planning Library;
Curator, Alexander Architectural Archive. Staff member since 1995.

AT A RECENT RECEPTION for an exhibit opening, a student asked me how long I had worked at the Architecture and Planning Library and Alexander Architectural Archive. "Since 1995," I replied. It seems not so long ago, but judging by the look on her young face, it must have measured nearly a lifetime. In an archive, it isn't unusual to think of a "lifetime" as a standard of measurement, and similarly, an archival collection is considered more valuable by the sum of its parts. It is desirable that an architect's collection reflect her multiple creative endeavors, and not just a single facet (imagine if all that remained from her records were her project specifications). Some of our finest collections provide records of built projects from the design stage through completion, both visual and textual, as well as from a variety of other activities including publishing,

working in professional associations, teaching, keeping diaries, and taking trip photos.

At the repository level, a strong architectural archive will reflect the many different roles related to design, including architecture, landscape, planning, interiors, and affiliated businesses, such as brick or terra cotta companies. For example, a scholar researching the Texas Instruments Semiconductor Building in Dallas (1958), recently found himself consulting five different archival collections, each reflecting a different contribution to the project: O'Neil Ford with his design and working drawings, Arch Swank's specifications and descriptions of the hyperbolic paraboloids, Richard Colley's early design concepts and presentation boards, and the records of planner Sam Zisman and landscape architect Dan Heyn. Part by part, each collection contributes and enriches the historic record for this project.

Additional strength lies in the consolidation of records for our region. It is inspiring to walk through our stacks, past the life works of Galveston's Nicolas Clayton, San Antonio's Ayres and Ayres, and Fort Worth's Sanguinet, Staats and Hedrick. These are the architects who helped build Texas and beyond.

The archive also serves as the official repository for the School of Architecture. Our relationship with the school is implicitly linked to the school's own dynamic and organic trajectories, and the documentation of its history is an ongoing challenge requiring the school and the archive to work in partnership.

It is fitting that the original core of the archive was collected by faculty, created by students, and driven by course requirements. In 1958, Professor Drury Blakeley Alexander began a personal collection of coursework produced by his students. He also had the foresight fifteen years later to salvage much earlier student work headed for the dumpster when the library had to quickly move from its Goldsmith location to Battle Hall. Eventually, he began accepting professional work offered as gifts to his students conducting historic research. Over the years, the archive has grown and now ranks as one of the largest architectural repositories in the country with nearly 1,900 linear feet of textual and photographic material and over a quarter of a million drawings.

Donors are the life-blood of the archive. They not only provide collection material, but also gifts of support and a network of contacts ready to offer assistance. Through conversations with donors, we learn stories about the projects that provide a rich context for their records. In turn, donors learn about the value and functions of an archive and understand the costs involved in stewardship. Many donors provide support for preservation supplies and labor so that their records can be processed quickly. This type of gift often supports graduate students, who gain valuable experience working directly with primary sources.

The archive deliberately continues on the trajectory of collecting, preserving, and making architectural records available for scholarship. These tasks are becoming more and more dominated by technological demands of expertise, new skill sets, and data storage, making our goals virtual moving targets. Technology changes the process of record production and, ultimately, how and what is collected, making it difficult to identify and preserve records for future generations.

Technology has completely revolutionized how users find archival collections. In 1995, the archive was a nearly all-analog unit. Handwritten card files, forms, key-typed inventories, and a few electronic word-processing files formed the finding aids to the collections. Archivists practiced very few standards in creating finding aids. Simply put, users had little control over how, when, and what to expect while conducting primary research. About ten years ago, technological standards were developed for encoding data elements in the finding aids. This facilitated two major advances: publication of finding aids on the web and the ability to search for specific types of information, for instance an architect's name, across multiple finding aids in a single search. The impact was felt immediately, as scholars could conduct preliminary research online and learn about our collections. The archive began receiving more visitors from out of the country, lending higher visibility for the school internationally. Today, every collection in the archive has a web presence. All finding aids are now available via the library's online catalog and in Texas Archival Resources Online (TARO), a web-based service where one can search across participating Texas repositories in a single federated search. Finding aid records are also submitted to national and international archival reference databases such as ArchiveGrid and Archive Finder.

On the other hand, technology has brought about unrecoverable losses of architectural records. Architects have shifted from analog to digital media, and the archive will soon see the results. An architectural record is fast becoming something that is not always printed or drawn on a piece of paper. Firms are no longer keeping clipping files, nor are they corresponding on impressively designed letterhead or producing piles of hand-rendered design schemes on trace. Now they browse the web for reference, correspond via email and online social networks, continuously overlay their designs using proprietary software, and produce 3-D digital representations. Scholars are losing evidence of context and the evolution of design. Areas once rich in documentation are left empty with deleted email and project versions never saved. Although the archive's mission remains unchanged, the paths to identifying, acquiring, and preserving archival material and making such records available to our public are much different.

Archives are struggling with technical issues of how to preserve the look, feel, and functionality of complex files like those created in Building Information Modeling (BIM) software. Archives also are trying to learn how to capture and provide descriptive metadata including original file format information. Questions arise about keeping these files renderable, readable, and accessible while ensuring their integrity. Preservation issues are moving from the fragility of paper fibers to easily corruptible bit streams. The limits of electronic data storage must now be considered along with the continuing demands for physical space to accommodate other modern records.

With these challenges come opportunities for new ways for the school and the archive to collaborate. The Texas Digital Libraries is already offering services, such as the Open Journal System, a vehicle where faculty can create electronically published peer review journals. The University of Texas Digital Repository is also available as a vehicle to receive faculty and student work, including CAD files, making it immediately available worldwide. These types of venues can provide access to collections and also streamline scholarship, including faculty-sponsored and student-curated exhibits and publications, resulting from research in the archive. There is also a research opportunity in the possibility of expanding the model of the Philadelphia Architects and Buildings project to produce a web-based clearinghouse on Texas architecture that would bring together relevant archival collections from around the world. Finally, there needs to be a strategy for preserving the electronic records of the school. Future trajectories will eventually become traces.

The school, its alumni, and the archive share many of the same challenges. Alumni and the archive can help each other discover ways to handle digital records. Integrating information literacy into the curriculum helps information professionals and faculty keep pace with each other and respond to changes in research and teaching. Our trajectories lead naturally to collaboration. In the archive, there is great value in the sum of its parts. Just as the collections interlock, so do the people of the archive—staff, researchers, donors—and the School of Architecture.

The Visual Resources Collection: Building an Image Collection for the 21st Century

Elizabeth Schaub, Director, Visual Resources Collection since 1997.
Joan Winter, Graduate Research Assistant (Information Studies), Visual Resources Collection

ESTABLISHED IN THE MID-1960s, the School of Architecture's Visual Resources Collection (VRC) serves as a repository for both analog and digital images that reflect the collective gaze of generations of faculty members and students. The collection documents sites that impelled someone to pick up a camera and photograph a building's facade or interior, a cityscape or landscape, or a particularly arresting detail. This visual record has become a resource for professors and students influencing future architects, planners, preservationists, critics, interior designers, landscape architects, and historians.

While the VRC's collection continues to expand in the digital age to meet the unique needs of the school's faculty and students, so does the myth that everything, no matter how obscure, can be found online on the open web and that institutionally supported collections are no longer an essential pedagogical resource. This mindset has the potential to jettison us back in time to the latter part of the 20th century when faculty and students developed their own slide collections—often with overlapping scope and limited access—instead of supporting a vision for a collectively built, centrally managed, sustainable and accessible digital image collection for the 21st century. To date, the VRC has developed a growing collection of digital images numbering over 80,000 files that require more than a terabyte of storage space.

In the digital age, we are reminded of the importance of collaboration, of emphasizing community over the isolated individual. The culture of sharing online is well established—as witnessed by the rise of social networks and the enthusiastic contribution of personal knowledge and content to sites like Wikipedia and Flickr. In the age of social networking, cloud computing, and crowd sourcing, institutional digital image collections are built collaboratively. Students receiving School of Architecture travel awards contribute photographs taken during their research trips, along with metadata describing their images, while others share images with one another and the world via the school's Flickr Group. In addition, faculty members with extensive slide collections and those who have transitioned to digital content donate their images and attendant metadata to the VRC.

Evolving with the digital revolution, the VRC is charged not only with growing and managing a digital collection but also with providing services supporting the use of digital image content, such as copyright tutorials and training on specialized presentation software.

The Digital Image Lifecycle

While it is easier and cheaper to take photographs than ever before, the thrill of instant gratification—of looking at a digital image and sharing it immediately after hitting the camera's shutter-release button—does not carry through to other parts of the digital image lifecycle.

Comparisons between analog and digital media are often influenced by the belief that digital content inherently saves time and money. While we have moved from the physical world of slides and their bulky storage cabinets to the immaterial and ephemeral realm of digital images, from being confined by a physical space to the infinite possibilities of an invisible bit stream, issues and challenges posed by our analog reality remain.

Digital images are fragile and require that attention be paid to ongoing issues such as storage and preservation. Just as important as the content are the words, also known as metadata, required to describe what is depicted in a digital image so that it may be easily found. The VRC's images are cataloged, stored, and preserved systematically, thus eliminating redundancies and ensuring the integrity of the content and its descriptive metadata not only in the present but also in the future.

Unique Image Content in the Visual Resources Collection

In October 2009, Flickr announced that it hosted over four billion images. It is easy to think that every image one might need for research can be found using a search engine like Google. However, retrieving classroom-ready, subject-specific digital images presents challenges.

Google is the gateway to a large but limited body of indexed content. Search engines do not search what is known as the Deep Web, i.e. the specialized databases and image collections most valuable to faculty and students.

As the VRC moves towards its fifth decade of existence, it is committed to collecting relevant images and to describe them in clear language so the university community can access high quality images to support their teaching and research needs. The collection contains difficult to find architectural plans, works outside the canon, locally focused collections, and ephemera. The ever-growing body of new architectural works demands that the VRC remain dedicated to the provision of visual documentation of both common tourist attractions and remote locations, in addition to regional and vernacular architecture.

The VRC is mining its slide holdings and reformatting unique materials in digital form to breathe new life into content that would otherwise go unused because of the adoption of digital technology. For example, the VRC's Hal Box and Logan Wagner Collection of Mexican Architecture and Urban Design numbers over 8,000 35mm slides photographed over a span of twelve years. Former School of Architecture Dean Hal Box and Dr. Logan Wagner, in collaboration with Earthwatch, an organization that provides volunteers for scholarly enterprises, documented communal open spaces built in Mexico from 2000 BC to the present. The VRC partnered with ARTstor, a growing image bank of nearly one million images for research and teaching. ARTstor provided funding for a graduate student hired by the VRC to process the collection and to digitize 5,732 slides over the course of seventy weeks. The VRC has continued to collaborate with ARTstor making a portion of the visual material collected and captured by the school's community, including images donated by professors Christopher Long and Wilfried Wang, available to ARTstor subscribers throughout the world.

The VRC also holds an extensive collection of images documenting the art and architecture of Texas, including the vernacular landscape, prominent buildings, and historically significant extant and demolished structures. A selection of slides, donated to the VRC by the estate of UT Professor of Art Marian B. Davis, includes images with a special emphasis on turn-of-the-century commercial architecture on Congress Avenue and 6th Street in Austin. With a grant from the university, the VRC partnered with the Alexander Architectural Archive to create *Texas Architecture: A Visual History*, a Web site providing access to images as well as a timeline of Texas architecture.

The collaborative relationships that the VRC has cultivated with the school's students are reflected in its holdings. Student-contributed images, from such places as India, Mongolia, Japan, and Brazil have been exhibited in the VRC, archived on the VRC's website, and made available as part of the VRC's permanent image collection.

With the rise of the internet as an immediate and ubiquitous way to communicate and share information, we have one foot in the digital and the other in the physical world. By ensuring that visual materials are accessible and of the highest quality, the VRC will continue to facilitate the use of images for communication and exploration, develop services to support the use of digital content, and preserve the collection for ongoing use in the future.

Visual Communication

Architectural education at UT is rooted in the art of drawing. The earliest form of instruction was an architectural drawing course offered by the College of Engineering in 1903. By 1910, the college had a School of Architecture and Drawing, which separated into a School of Architecture and a School of Drawing the following year. Course offerings in the early curricula included mechanical drawing—lettering, projective geometry, tinting, tracing, and blueprinting—and the traditional architectural drawing of plans, elevations, and sections.

Hugo Kuehne, who was interested in an artistic approach to design, established a three-year series of freehand drawing courses—the earliest visual communication sequence in the school. Students worked with mixed media, including pen, pencil, watercolor, and charcoal, to learn different visualization techniques. They used William J. Battle's casts and university campus buildings as sources to practice ornamental and figural detailing; live human models proved too scandalous for some university administrators but were used starting in the 1920s.

Visual communication education was directed by Raymond Everett during his thirty years of instruction. The Texas Rangers years brought about a major shift in the approach to visualization by introducing an emphasis on abstract composition manipulations and color theory. A collective use of traditional and progressive techniques has marked visual communication training thereafter.

Visual Communication in the BArch curriculum is currently part of a three-semester sequence that is closely integrated with the introductory architectural design studios. It provides students with a foundation in drawing, modeling, photography, and computer graphics. A similar series of courses is required in the MArch program. Undergraduate and graduate students alike complete their respective sequences with a formidable course on technical communication, in which they create CAD- or BIM-generated design development drawings. From the beginning, drawing has been taught alongside construction and theory as a tool for design.

Raymond Everett leads a student drawing session in front of the Hogg Auditorium and the Woman's Building (before 1948)

Students sit on the steps of Goldsmith Hall, drawing the Texas Union, 1963

Drawing on the steps between the West Mall Building and Goldsmith Hall, 1983

Left: Ray, Library
in Architecture
Building, undated

Right: Paul Eppes
(BArch '50), Sutton
Hall drawing:
Samuel Vosper,
critic, 1946

Right:
Raymond Everett

Below:
Watercolor of
the Architecture
Building courtyard,
1940s

RAYMOND EVERETT (1885-1948) was a painter, sculptor, and graphic artist who was the school's principal instructor of visual communication from his appointment in 1915 until his death. A native of New Jersey, he graduated with a BA from the Drexel Institute of Technology in 1906, where he studied under the illustrator Howard Pyle and then went on to earn a BS in Architecture from Harvard in 1909, studying with Joseph Lindon Smith and Denman Ross. Before joining the UTSOA faculty, Everett taught at Penn State University and the University of Michigan. While at UT he earned a MS in Architecture in 1931, submitting a thesis on his mural painting, "The March of Progress in Texas," which now hangs in the library of Webb Middle School in Austin. Everett taught a large range of topics, including drawing in various media, history of sculpture and painting, modeling, and material studies. While preferring conventional types of representation, he taught progressive courses on commercial art and advertising and plastic materials as applied to architecture. He encouraged students to engage the buildings and forms around them, even arranging field trips into the hills and country surrounding Austin. Everett's Texas landscape paintings are still prized by art collectors today.

Left: Kate Murphy (MArch '09), Reclining Nude, charcoal: Drawing 1, John Blood, critic, 2004

Right: Orville O. Rice (BArch '43), figure drawing, ca.1940

Upon hearing that a female architecture student had posed as a nude figure drawing model in 1927, UT President Benedict retorted that "this might do for Paris or Greenwich Village, but it cannot and will not be tolerated in Texas."

Students drawing from plaster cast collection, Engineering Building, ca.1916

Right: Alexis
Kurland,
jointed plywood
abstractions: Vertical
Studio, Joyce Rosner,
critic, 2008

Below: Michael
Borne (BArch '67),
material study, ink
line and watercolor:
Second Year,
Freehand Drawing,
Jorge Divino,
ca. 1964

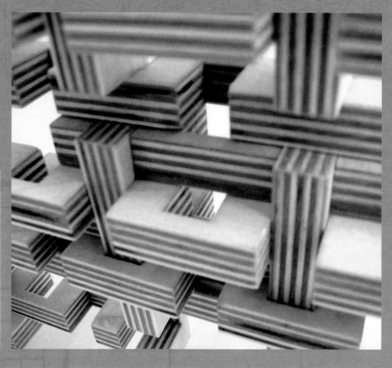

Left: Edna Ledesma
(MArch '10),
Tokyo Restaurant
Tower, pencil
and Photoshop:
Advanced Visual
Communication,
John Blood, 2010

Top Right: Kate
Murphy (MArch
'09), gouache and
watercolor study:
Europe Studio,
Larry Doll,
critic, 2008

Bottom Right:
Cy Wagner,
study for the
Prudential Group
in Detroit Michigan,
15-minute marker
drawing, 1975

Beginnings: Reflections on the
History of First-Year Design Education

Owen Cappleman, Associate Professor Emeritus. Faculty member 1964-2004.

AS RECENTLY AS THE LATE 1960s, first-year design (then called "Basic Design") in both the visual arts and in architecture at most universities was based on a common pedagogy inspired by the Bauhaus, and the faculty teaching the course in architecture as well as in art were usually artists, either painters or sculptors or, sometimes, graphic designers. This situation allowed me to be qualified for a teaching position in the School of Architecture in the fall of 1964, just three days after I had begun work on my master of fine arts degree in the then brand-new Art Building on the other side of campus.

Within a few years of beginning my university teaching career, some first-year-design faculty began to question the relevance and efficacy of this model of introductory design, which was purely visual in nature and, to some of us, very superficial and often irrelevant. There were heated discussions over replacing it with a "systems" orientation that incorporated functional analysis, identification of required conditions, and establishment of performance criteria. Ironically, those favoring the latter were the young artists, while those defending the continuation of the visual arts approach were the older, more established architects. Eventually, with contributions by other then-new faculty including Richard Dodge, Gerlinde Leiding, and Dick Oliver, and the encouragement of "old-timer" Richard Swallow, we set about revamping the content and instruction of first-year design based on the systems model, which continued to evolve through the 1970s.

In 1980, Michael Jordan left Auburn University and joined the UTSOA faculty. He and I began a fertile working partnership, and our "one + one = three" symbiosis resulted in a revolutionary transformation of first-year pedagogy that received national and, eventually, international attention. We revisited and edited the old Bauhaus studies to search for the fundamental aspects of that approach that truly related to architecture and updated them with particular attention to proportion and scale. Scalar concerns emphasized the "human use of the built environment" at all scales from that of the object through residential to monumental to urban scale. Whatever the subject matter or content of the project, which could take several weeks to complete, we would begin with two-dimensional configurations that soon moved into the third (and sometimes fourth) dimension, all the while operating under carefully devised parameters. The 3-D iteration, while at first abstract, would transform at some point into a piece of the built environment realized at a specific scale.

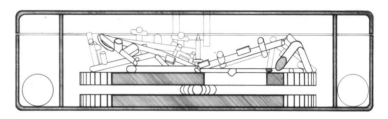

Perhaps our most satisfying project was based on the work of artist Joseph Cornell, who produced mysterious—often mystical—boxes made of found materials. After completing a series of two-dimensional projects and then engaging in intense study of the artist and his work, each student was asked to create his or her own "Cornellesque" box. The two major philosophical tenets that we stressed in this project were "seek the unexpected" and "do not be precious with your work." To these ends, upon completion and critique of the student boxes, we took them to the woodshop where each box was sawed in half. Not only did this brutal act bring to an abrupt end any feeling of preciousness the students had about their creation, it allowed them to look inside the box from a totally unanticipated point of view. Working from this new resource, we completed the project by generating A Commemorative Pavilion for Joseph Cornell.

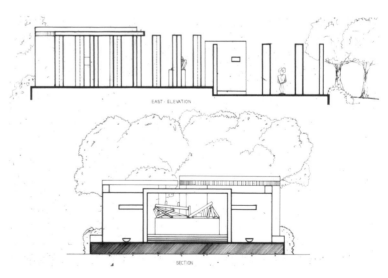

Yu-Wen Diana Huang (BSID '93), Joseph Cornell Box and Pavilion Exercise: First-year Design, Owen Cappleman, critic, 1991

Beyond our curricular revisions, Jordan's and my two most significant accomplishments were the establishment of a unique computer laboratory and the development of an international network of beginning design educators that culminated in the publication of a book. The former stemmed from the National Architectural Accreditation Board's assessment of the

Yu-Wen Diana
Huang (BSID),
Joseph Cornell
Box and Pavilion
Exercise: First-year
Design, Owen
Cappleman, critic,
1991

school in 1985, which gave high praise to our first-year program but noted that computing was noticeably absent in all subject areas. Jordan and I took that criticism as a personal challenge.

Within six months we garnered grants from the IBM Corporation and the university administration that allowed us to create what was then the world's only First-Year Design Computer Imaging Lab. The lab opened on a limited basis in the spring of 1987 and was fully operational by the following fall. It was reported in national computing magazines and prompted invitations for us to speak at conferences across the United States and even abroad. One of the highlights of my career was to be keynote presenter at an international first-year design conference in Istanbul.

The book developed along an entirely different track. Over the years, Jordan and I had solicited sample first-year design project statements from colleagues at universities all over the country. We photocopied and stapled them together with a cover sheet declaring them the "Best Beginning Design Projects" and mailed a copy to each contributor. The first two of these were produced under the watchful eye of Tim McGinty, then teaching at Arizona State University, who functioned as organizer, editor, and publisher.

When we were thinking about initiating a third edition, we got the idea to expand the concept in the following ways: 1) turn the solicitation process into a competition; 2) go international with our search; and 3) seek a publisher to produce a real book rather than a stapled set of photocopies. Our plan was to write approximately three-fourths of the text and then stage a conference with the contributors selected from the competition, which attracted entries from as far away as India, China, and Australia, and as near as College Station.

The school generously supported our effort, and to our great surprise and delight not only did the North American contributors attend, but the majority of the foreign contributors did as well. This three-day affair was so rich and informative that after the dust had settled, we discarded everything we had previously written and started all over again. The book, entitled *Foundations in Architecture: An Annotated Anthology of Beginning Design Projects*, was released in December of 1993 by Van Nostrand Reinhold. Part of our contract dictated—at our insistence—that the design of the entire book was to be done by Jordan and me. And it was. Although long out of print, it continues to be of value to readers. A recent glimpse at Amazon.com showed five copies for sale with prices averaging from three to almost seven times its original cost!

My long tenure at UT not only generated exciting studio learning experiences for the students, a unique working relationship, an innovative freshman computer imaging lab, and a very special book, but it ultimately helped to produce a number of outstanding architects including Stanley Haas (BArch '73), Evan Taniguchi (attended '72-'77), Mary Hardin (BArch '79, MArch '83), Fred Clarke (BArch '70), and Hans and Torrey Butzer (both BArch '90), to name just a few. This forty-year journey was rewarding beyond belief. And if, as many say, "teaching is learning," then I may well be among the most learned folks around.

In the Spirit of the Texas Rangers

Smilja Milovanovic-Bertram, Associate Professor. Faculty member since 1983.

IN THE YEARS BETWEEN 1951 AND 1956, a group of young architects, later termed the Texas Rangers— Bernhard Hoesli, Colin Rowe, John Hejduk, Robert Slutzky, Lee Hodgden, John Shaw, Lee Hirsche, and Werner Seligmann—set about creating a new design curriculum for the School of Architecture that emphasized space over form.[1] Students visualized space through use of both two-dimensional and three-dimensional exercises informed by phenomenology and Rowe and Slutzky's theory of transparency. History provided precedents as idea generators. Context became an important architectural consideration, and regionalism was seen as a force impacting design. Design process was emphasized. Drawing studios and color theory were instrumental in teaching students to "see." Theory-based lectures augmented design studios to "feed the mind and imagination."[2]

In this studio environment, John Hejduk devised his "Nine Square Grid Exercise," based on a composition of nine squares forming a framework for design investigations. Introduced in 1954, it became very important as a means of introducing basic design as a kit of parts exercise. He followed up the exercise with a series of studies (1954-63) called the "Texas Houses" project, all based on a nine-square grid. Hejduk further explored the nine-square grid exercise as a first-year

Daniel Morrison, Video Gallery: Design II, Smilja Milovanovic-Bertram, critic, 2008

study when he joined the faculty at Cooper Union in 1964.[3] Over the years, many schools of architecture have adapted the exercise in some form and continue to use it as a point of departure in design studios.

The legacy of the Texas Rangers at the UTSOA may be seen in four aspects of the school's current pedagogy for the foundation years. First, their point, line, plane exercises remain in use today as well as the genesis pedagogy derived from Theo van Doesburg's space-time construction and Gestalt psychology. A second link is the use of precedent as a means to inform design. Modernism is not viewed as separate from history; it

Daniel Morrison, Line-Square-Rectangle 3-D Composition: Design I, Joyce Rosner, critic, 2007

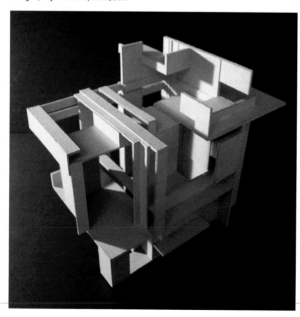

is a continuation of it. Critical to the shaping of this attitude was Colin Rowe's essay, "The Mathematics of the Ideal Villa" (1947) where Palladio's Villa Malcontenta was as contemporary as Le Corbusier's Villa Stein in his analysis. Third, context and regionalism are equally important as idea generators. In 1957 Rowe wrote an article in *Architectural Forum* titled "Lockhart, Texas," comparing the landscape around Austin to that of Tuscany and southern France. The Texas Rangers' critical assessment of nearby towns, such as Lockhart and Lampasas, became the context for studio projects, and those sites continue to be studied today.[4] Finally, a fourth link is the act of embracing art in all its components (painting, cinematography, photography) as part of the architectural dialogue just as Slutzky and Lee Hirsche, students of Josef Albers, merged painting and architecture in the design studios.

The Curriculum Today:
Design I Studio, Fall Semester

Design I introduces the student to the basic elements of architecture. Employing two- and three-dimensional techniques of composition, it aims, through the construction and discussion of formal studies, to build a refined language of spatial definition, organization, and occupation. The work of the semester begins with studies of two-dimensional compositions as organizational systems, which then lead to three-dimensional studies of form, space, light, and occupation. The process requires of each student careful first-hand observation and a disciplined approach toward the act of making. Each project or exercise builds upon the previous one, requiring the students to work through a series of progressive physical studies toward the development of an architectural idea. The projects and exercises explored in Design I are intended to provide the student with foundations in the conceptual, perceptual, and tectonic skills necessary for subsequent design work in architecture/interior design. Sequentially linked projects are used to introduce a formal language of architecture, concluding with the more performative fundamentals of scale, light, and gravity. Design studios and visual communications are taught as complements, side by side. Visual communication studios reinforce the design studio by teaching students how to visualize their ideas.

Design II Studio, Spring Semester

The second semester's studies are titled Analysis + Context + Production. In this semester students begin to apply an understanding of design within the context of the built environment. Point, line, and plane are now understood as column, beam or wall, for example —or place, path, and threshold—and are also engaged within the context of time and space through climate, materiality, perception, and precedent. Students consider the implications of context within and between different scales, including the intimate scale of the detail and of the body, and the larger scales of building, landscape, and urban environments. To do this, students must first understand the various components of the built environment and the relationships between them (architectonics). This is achieved through analysis as a process of investigation by taking things apart, physically and conceptually, at different scales and through different mediums. Students then practice putting things together through production, as an iterative process of weaving and folding.

UTSOA and ETH-Zurich

Bernhard Hoesli left UT in 1957 and eventually returned to his native Switzerland where he joined the faculty of the Eidgenössische Technische Hochschule Zürich (ETH). He introduced the pedagogy of the Texas Rangers, and today, as at the UTSOA, aspects of it survive, if somewhat muted.[5] Exercises are still structured to create an interactive heuristic approach to problem solving. Process is not a means to an established end. A broad synopsis of how the application of Hoesli's vision has evolved begins with the emphasis on space rather than form. In the 1960s, the emphasis at the ETH became the continuity of space. The 1970s saw a shift at both the ETH and the UTSOA from form as means to process as form (see Owen Cappleman's essay, "Beginnings," also in this book). Today (particularly at the ETH), priority is given to the purposeful dematerialization of form through machinic processes. In the ETH model, process becomes disciplining—a discursive practice using

reasoning and argument, not intuition. Diagramming is a significant component of the ETH process/discipline. This is both machinic and recursive in nature, branching into new alternatives. Perhaps because of its technical nature, the ETH uses a more compressed timeline than the UTSOA for student assimilation of the complexities of design processes.

The UTSOA still uses a sequence of point-line-plane to 3-D studies of form, space, light, and occupation very much in the manner of Hoesli and the Texas Rangers in the first (fall) semester. The ETH on the other hand, assigns a smaller role to Hoesli's notion of space in the first semester. The two programs are more similar in the contents of the second (spring) semester exercises in analysis, context, and production, and they both address urban form in an architectural project. Differences are apparent in the ETH's considerable emphasis on technology in these early semesters, far beyond the UTSOA's curriculum at present. Analysis of precedent occurs in both schools, although the UTSOA presents it in the second semester. Both schools emphasize this analysis as a means to move away from the original canonic building.

The current state of architectural practice is specialized and fragmented by sub-disciplines in which new technology, digital tools, and concerns for sustainability provide a somewhat different framework through which design considerations are filtered than in the 1950s. The architectural quest now at both institutions is to view and manipulate space from multiple points simultaneously in new material and digital settings. Despite the changes, the study of the nature of space remains a central focus of the foundation years in an architect's education. For this inquiry, the basic exercises the Texas Rangers developed at the UTSOA nearly sixty years ago are still relevant as pedagogy.

[1] This essay has been drawn from a longer discussion of the legacy of Bernhard Hoesli at the School of Architecture and the ETH. See Smilja Milovanovic-Bertram, "In the Spirit of the Texas Rangers," 24th National Conference on the Beginning Design Student, College of Architecture, Georgia Institute of Technology, Atlanta, Georgia, March 13-16, 2008: http://smartech.gatech.edu/handle/1853/29118.

[2] Alexander Caragonne, *The Texas Rangers: Notes from an Architectural Underground* (Cambridge, MA: MIT Press, 1995), 7.

[3] John Hejduk, *Education of an Architect, a Point of View: The Cooper Union School of Art and Architecture 1964-1971* (1971) reprint (New York: Monecelli, 2000).

[4] See Caragonne, 249-254.

[5] See Liat Uziyel, ed., *Inchoate: An Experiment in Architectural Education* (Zurich: ETH and Barcelona: Actar, 2003).

To Draw or Not to Draw

Nichole Wiedemann, Associate Dean for Undergraduate Programs, Associate Professor. Faculty member since 1997.

Thursday, January 28, 2010, 8:45 a.m.
Goldsmith Hall 2.110

In Visual Communication II, seventy architecture and interior design undergraduates sit in groups on cubes, chairs, and the floor balancing their drawing boards with paper, ink, brush, quill, stick, and a cup of water. At the center of each gathering is a bird to be closely observed and, later, to be researched. Two instructors, Danelle Briscoe and I, as well as three graduate teaching assistants, Katherine Lee, Mike Start, and Beau Frail, wander the room squeezing through what space is left.

The students proceed with the assignment for today: fifteen minutes of making thick and thin, light and dark lines in ink with quill, brush, and stick; fifteen minutes of

gestural sketches superimposing ten views of the bird on one sheet using stick or quill; fifteen minutes of gestural sketches superimposing ten views of the bird on one sheet using brush; fifteen minutes of introduction to ink wash techniques; forty-five minutes using line and wash techniques to explore texture and pattern of plumage; and thirty minutes to discuss successes and failures in ink/ink wash techniques and to introduce the next assignment.

The collection of birds—thirty-nine specimens in plastic tubes or naturally poised from the Texas Natural History Collections—provides the lens to explore the ecology of our region in Central Texas. Concurrently in Design II, the

students study the migration patterns, physiology, habitats, and behaviors. The insights gathered from these initial studies create the rich context for the design of a bird blind and birding center at Hornsby Bend. Environmental forces, including light, wind, and water, inspire both pragmatic and poetic responses in the designs.

Next Tuesday...

One hundred years after the university first offered a degree in architecture, we are still teaching students to draw—to make marks or lines on a surface (by hand). In the first-year undergraduate curriculum, every Tuesday and Thursday (with over 160 contact hours and two or three times that in homework), we instruct students on manual techniques and media of the discipline. One might wonder why we still invest so much time in the instruction of hand drawing when our graduates enter a predominantly digital, professional environment? Why do we continue to deem drawing essential to the education of an architect and interior designer in our undergraduate degree requirements?

Drawing is an experiment with reality, an act of invention, which cannot be recreated entirely by other means. The design student starts his or her education by learning to utilize the tools of the discipline: pencil, paper, parallel bar, triangle, ink, watercolor, brush, pastel, charcoal, eraser, as well as glue, board, scale, straight edge, wood, and, later, mouse, laser cutter, CNC router, and 3-D printer. From the viewpoint of students, these instruments are ways to extract and illustrate the multitude of designs that already exist in their heads; in other words, they are tools of reaffirmation. However, it is through the act of making,

through drawing in particular, that the students are liberated from their preconceptions.

Drawing necessitates intimacy and distance, simultaneously. Observational drawing teaches a student to absorb the object, whether bird, building, or landscape, with the eyes. An intimacy, or closeness, unites the subject and object during the process of drawing and, consequently, transforms the student's awareness. Measure is established through comparison rather than by unit. Space is defined and full rather than empty. Form is a consequence of light and shade. The presumably known becomes unknown and known again as the drawing materializes from the white of the page. As a heightened perception is gained, an ambiguity is retained. Omissions and oversights reflect conscious, or unconscious, interests of the student. Through drawing, the object of study—thing or idea—is no longer distinct from the subject. The student and bird, for instance, emerge as one, inseparable.

Drawing opens a space of translation. As the sculptor learns from the stone by the touch of the hand, the student learns through the actions of his or her hands. The sculptor's hand feels the fissure in the stone and instinctively guides the initial concept in another, more accommodating, direction. For the designer, the complexities of space are tested as two lines meet on the page; questions arise as to the quality and material of these marks as they strive to define monumentality, intimacy, efficacy, movement, and so on. As if in a clandestine conversation, the hands and eyes have the ability to guide the intellect to unanticipated solutions by asking involuntary questions.

Left: Colin Rowe conducting desk crits

Right: Student working on bird assignment: Visual Communication II, Nichole Wiedemann and Danelle Briscoe, critics, 2010

Review of bird
assignment: Visual
Communications II,
Nichole Wiedemann
and Danelle Bris-
coe, critics, 2010

This tactile knowledge cannot occur before the making begins, before the pencil, or any other implement is engaged and the space delineated. Ultimately, the act of drawing helps to replace the naïve images of architecture and interior design (what it looks like), with the pursuit for ideas (how is it meaningful) and performances (what it does). With such understanding, a door is no longer a door but a threshold between inside and outside, between public and private, between body and city, between light and dark or just between —a liminal space to be occupied. Through the process of drawing, the door is unmade and becomes charged with potential, existing simultaneously as question and answer. Discovery takes place during an oscillating process of making and unmaking, and in a way, the product is inconsequential. Ultimately, drawing doesn't teach students to draw, it teaches them to see and think.

To draw or not to draw? How can we not?

Tuesday, February 16, 2010, 9:10 a.m.
Goldsmith Hall 2.110

Problem 4, titled "birdPATTERN," using watercolor, is reviewed. Using color juxtaposition, layering, and saturation, the objectives are to introduce "transparency" as a way to generate spatial qualities that are both explicit and implicit.

While gaining competency with color theory and watercolor techniques, the students continued a discussion that began here in the 1960s by faculty members Robert Slutzky and Colin Rowe. (The reference, lost on the 2010 freshman class, will soon have meaning and resonance as they move forward in their architectural history sequence.) At the same time, the students contributed to a new discourse by engaging the resurgence of "pattern," "variation," and, even, "biomimicry," terms currently aligned with contemporary digital discourse.

Next Thursday...

Drawing Now And Then

Danelle Briscoe, Assistant Professor. Faculty member since 2009.

FOR MOST ARCHITECTS, drawing is not a hobby that happens occasionally or "now and then." Instead, it is an indispensable act of abstraction that we often use more than words—an act capable of communicating our every design idea and thought. Regardless of whether done manually, computer-translated, or computer-generated, drawing essentially equates to design. The modes by which drawings are now executed might impose a change in how we draw, but not necessarily what we draw. The appreciation of content over technique, whether done by hand or digital medium, is what continues to distinguish our School of Architecture in this digital age, just as it did then when I received my bachelor of architecture in 1995.

Like Austin, the school was a smaller and less populated place in the early 1990s; with degree programs only in Architecture and Community and Regional Planning. A small portion of the Sutton basement was converted to a computer lab in 1993, and for many students software was just emerging as a design tool in the studio. Michael Benedikt (First Conference in Cyberspace, May 1990) and Marcos Novak (Director of the Advanced Design Research Program) were positioning the school at the forefront of digital architecture and led the discipline in a discourse on cyberspace. This occurrence afforded students an opportunity to design and think about space as derived from and inhabited in the virtual space of the computer. Despite the increasing ubiquity of CAD, studio

drawing during these years was primarily done with pencil or ink on paper. Minor changes meant erasing and redrawing, while major changes often meant recreating the drawing from scratch. This invaluable hand process for such design delivery taught to us by professors like John Blood, Richard Dodge, and Richard Swallow, fostered a commitment of thoughtfulness and sensibility of creation. Through this dichotomy of drawing and design praxis, there was, if nothing else, a sense of optimism about negotiating the material and immaterial mediums and methods in the school.

As testimony to this perception, Chris Roach (BArch '95), now in his second year at Harvard University's Graduate School of Design, remembers Novak's Music of Architecture: Computation and Composition and David Heyman's Site Design as the more memorable courses of his undergraduate experience, or at least ones he finds himself continually returning to. "Somehow these courses managed to plant the seeds in my head that have grown into the structure of my own particular frame of reference for understanding architecture and the arts."

Novak's seminar was appreciated not so much for the proto-cyber-architecture that some people associated with it (and which he heavily de-emphasized) but more for the way the course introduced a different way of thinking about design. The examples shown in the class, from Iannis Xenakis to John Cage to Marcel Duchamp, helped introduce the kinds of avant-garde design practices that continue to resonate within architectural discourse today. Mark Gonzales (BArch '95) also recalls Novak's seminar:

The first night of the course, he spent 60 minutes reading one of Cage's 'poems' aloud to us. To call it a poem is a bit of a stretch, because it was basically random words out of the dictionary, i.e. 'cat lunch enormous attitude luxury data tree sewer phone car ...' for 60 minutes! I would look at Meg (Wilson, BArch '95) and we'd give each other esoteric glances like 'is this guy for real?' Ultimately though, I think I got more out of the course as time went on - even years after I left UT.

Matthew Priest (BArch '96), now practicing with WRT Solomon E.T.C. in San Francisco, took the Trans-Architecture studio with Novak and strongly remembers an hour-long discourse surprisingly about traditional detailing of openings, such as doors and windows. Novak started with the fairly obvious part about how trim was developed to cover joints between dissimilar materials, but then took it in a direction about fractals and such, to the effect that each time another layer of detail was introduced, it effectively multiplied the richness of the detail. At some point, this was all tied into the "economy of bits" in the early digital age (when dial-up was still the burgeoning means for internet access).

In 1995, when Novak wrote "Transmitting Architecture: The Transphysical City," the World Wide Web was still a novelty and the home computer was not yet ubiquitous. The consideration of architecture as something that could be transmitted—literally, not just metaphorically—was unheard of. At the time, putting the word "transmitting" next to the word "architecture" was madness itself, just as phrasing "liquid architectures" had been before it. And yet, like "liquid architectures," it was a prescient idea. As a graduating class, we all agreed Novak was well ahead of his time and that his thoughts were likely prophetic.

Now, fifteen years later, a shift in the discipline's relationship to digital architecture has taken place— from purely formal and virtual experiments to a more pragmatic interest in the optimization of geometry through processes that integrate the digital and the analog, or the everyday and the fantastic.[1] At present, the basement of Sutton is a fully digital resource—not only with regard to how drawings are created and output, but with technologies capable of 3-D printing or scanning a model in order to make real what at one time lived only in virtual reality. The relationship between architectural drawing and production is being brought closer together, given the fluidity and accuracy of digital tools, such as CNC mills and laser-cutters. Computer-aided manufacturing processes provide means to "draw" out new architectural ideas and challenge traditional methods of project delivery.

In a time when the computer is a familiar fixture in the studio space, the school is fortunate to still have John Blood offering courses in design drawing. As well, the legacy of avant-garde thinking remains evident with Michael Benedikt. Design studios and seminars punctuate workflows with the breathless announcement of yet another paradigm shift of parametric modeling of information and fabrication as design tools. Again, parametric thinking imposes a change in how we draw, not what we draw. The parameters one creates to formulate a design exist apart from hand or digital means. Does an amalgam of manual and digital methodologies muddy the clarity of material and immaterial spaces, and thus result (to quote Michael Benedikt) in an "infected middle" that tries to span both worlds? Recognition of the apparent schism is to realize that its resolution lies within the continued exploration and practice of architecture.

A Materials Lab now resides in the West Mall Building and affirms the school's commitment to return a sense of materiality to an immaterial realm. Alongside samples of every conceivable material, ongoing exhibitions fill the space with design studio work and research. In the fall of 2009, "Constructions in PAPER" displayed laser cut iterative contributions from the studios of Assistant Professors Michael Beaman, Igor Siddiqui, and me. The exhibition demonstrated how drawings can now be cut and assembled.

For Novak, now teaching at the University of California, Santa Barbara, "Transmitting Architecture" has evolved as well:

If, in 1995 it was understood to mean using artificial algorithms to create artificial worlds, today it means making use of the natural algorithms that are already acting directly in the world, being smarter, more balanced, more flexible, and more robust. It means that what is to be transmitted must be more like a request for proposals and collaborations among peers than like an ultimatum issued among unequals.

In this period of digital embrace, the school's studio space has held sacred the parallel bar and the modeling table. The belief that architecture must be grounded in space, light, materials, and context, should not deny that these premises can be achieved through a collaborative digital process. Some students come to the school with digital media skills already in tow, some are autodidacts, and a large number are waiting to be taught. The future of digital tools depends on the degree to which the academy can accept the proposition that exemplary architectural design can be created in a computer-mediated environment and that digital thinking is indeed architectural thinking.

In response to Peter Eisenman's lecture "On Lateness and the Politics of Surface," Novak writes:

It's never too late to be early, but to be early, one must first belong to one's time. Being born in a certain period does not guarantee this. Most people live in the past (in all but some small fractions of their lives, if that). Becoming contemporary requires great discipline and extended effort, not to mention a substantial amount of good fortune. Once one has achieved becoming contemporary, though, being early simply means this: one stands firmly at the present, faces forward, sees, thinks, imagines, and leaps as far into the future as possible.[2]

The School of Architecture has always positioned itself to not simply accept the inevitability of a technological imperative. That critical stance better frames for its students a working methodology for contemporary architectural design and the future.

[1] Danelle Briscoe, "Practically Digital," in *Digital Architecture and Construction*, A. Ali and C. A. Brebbia, eds. (Southhampton, UK: WIT Press, 2006), 111-120.

[2] Marcos Novak, "Prologomenon: Transmitting Architecture Revisited. On the Occasion of the XXIII UIA World Congress, 2008," in *USC Architecture IDNWS* [University of Southern California] (Spring 2010), 27.

Gentlemen Do [Not] Operate Machinery: A Few Thoughts on Technology, Knowledge, and Craft

Michael Leighton Beaman, Assistant Professor. Faculty member since 2007.

IN THE LATE 1980s, an early attempt to incorporate computation in design education was undertaken at the Harvard Graduate School of Design.[1] It did not go well. Rather than directly and intuitively creating and manipulating points, lines, surfaces, and solids as the majority of computer aided design (CAD) users experience this interaction today, students were asked to engage in the actual coding process. Moving back and forth between the formal and physical languages of architecture and the coded language of programming proved difficult. However, what proved insurmountable was validating this conceptual shift in the location of craft for a discipline dependent on individual design processes. Malcolm McCullough, one of the developers of CAD systems, has noted that the viewpoint taken by a majority of faculty and students at the time was that "gentlemen did not operate machinery."[2]

With the advent of CAD, computer numerical controlled (CNC) manufacturing, and, more recently, data-driven design parametics, the conception, definition, development, communication, and production of the objects and spaces we create has shifted the location of technology from an extra-architectural position. Crafting architecture at the level of protocol/procedure through computation and algorithm has become more accessible to architects closing the gap between intuitive and rigorous design processes that was so troubling to the discipline thirty years ago. Whether it is form, data, performance, material, assembly, analysis, visualization, or production, computation offers a multiplicity of trajectories, as well as hurdles, for the future of thinking and making in architecture.

What follows are a few thoughts on why, now, in 2010, architecture, especially in academia, continues to struggle to find a level of comfort and kinship with technology—more importantly, why, despite that discomfort, and largely because of it, the discipline offers a perfect platform for collaboration with technology.

The Value of Discomfort

Though the course at Harvard was an early attempt to develop computational knowledge through digital technology within architectural education, it was by far not the first. Computational paradigms for design have had many beginnings. Here at the School of Architecture in the 1950s, the Texas Rangers played a significant role in establishing an abstract and analytical approach to design by way of diagrams and rules through the idea of the model.[3] Though this agenda did not rely on digital technologies directly, conceptually, it established a pedagogy through which architects, researchers, and educators could develop digital design practices and helped lay the academic groundwork of algorithmic and computational approaches to design. By the early 1970s, George Stiny and James Gips had developed shape grammars, a computational drawing process.[4] Shape grammars, the predominant language upon which much of Harvard's course was based, owed its formal development to the approach taken by the Rangers.

In the 1980s, Carnegie Mellon University incorporated computer programming course work into almost every discipline. UCLA, MIT, and a number of other universities were developing research and education with computation and digital visualization during this time as well. The 1990s saw an explosion of production and theory along this trajectory. Though the implications on education and practice were just forming, small pockets of faculty and students were braving new terrain at many universities. Still, just as the trend toward incorporating computation in architectural education was being forged, difficulties and push-back similar to those experienced at Harvard occurred on many university campuses.

McCullough implies two things in his characterization of faculty and students at Harvard at the time. The first is an assumption on the part of many in academia and practice that a dichotomy exists between technological development and architectural knowledge and that technology lies somewhere outside the boundaries of the discipline of architecture. One could use technology as a tool, appropriate its products, or theorize its impact, but it was still machinery. Second, in using the word "gentlemen," McCullough emphasizes a different knowledge by class (not necessarily gender). Architecture, along with most professional disciplines, had separated the "traditional relationship between producer and means of production," stripping itself of the need to engage machines to create knowledge.[5] Clearly, this was an endeavor that did not belong in the realm of academia.

This devalued and estranged relationship between technology and architecture is an interesting one in that it can be traced to the development of architecture itself as an autonomous discipline: first, in architecture's separation from the act of building; then, from fine arts, engineering, and, finally, mechanical technologies. As the built environment became more complex, the outsourcing of knowledge and craft increased. Architecture slowly shed responsibilities, floating between being general in breadth and instructional in effect. Generally, this estranged relationship has roots in how we have come to conceptualize and categorize knowledge and craft within most, if not all, of our professional disciplines: knowledge lies with the creator, craft with the means of production.

Architecture is unlike many other professions. It already provides a historical basis to collaborate with other disciplines for expertise and with other industries, while remaining tethered to its origins. However, the professional and academic mainstream has become comfortable with merely appropriating technology for its own pursuits. Though knowledge and craft in the form of design and building continues to be the point of emphasis for academia, knowledge and craft in the form of technology has not. This has not always been the case, and need not be the case for the future. Discomfort is healthy, but disengagement is dangerous, precisely because it erodes the exceptional power of the discipline by reducing its efficacy and relevance. Fortunately, attempts to construct a collaborative agenda for architectural and technological development are already part of the scope of the discipline. Computational paradigms are not foreign entities; they have grown out of the theoretical development of the discipline.

An Ideal Platform

The machine leads to the device, to the gadget, and to a manner of thinking by which the hinge becomes far more expressive than the door — Peter Cook[6]

Architecture (and design in general) remains uniquely defined among professional disciplines. Architecture requires abstraction in thought—the ability to provide organizational and conceptual frameworks to the design and implementation of constructed environments, while simultaneously requiring knowledge of craft to form the very objects and effects that constitute those constructed environments. And as such, architects reconcile knowledge and craft into an indivisible and plastic construct.

Having to navigate a sea of possibilities is a good problem to have. In what other discipline can unchecked exploration and critical thinking push against one another in such a way as to produce new knowledge from uncertain potential? The will of the discipline to expand and contract the bounds of its own definition is precisely what makes technological collaboration such a necessary problem for us to engage. It speaks to the very heart of what it means to design. More importantly, the continuous development of the plastic

relationship between craft and knowledge through these very manifestations of uncertainty is what makes architecture a platform like no other. We should not consider technology as a thing we consume, but a thing we help shape. What architecture offers technological development is a platform on which to be experimental and critical simultaneously.

As institutions of higher learning grapple with how and on what terms we should address these concerns, it is in many cases students and young practitioners who are the least tentative about exploration. Because of this, much of the transformative research into computation and practice is taking place outside of academia. Colin Rowe some years after his time at UT provided a simple critique of architectural education and why it is such a unique and powerful platform for collaboration. His charge to educators in 1980 speaks well to our concerns today if we replace his phrase "modern architecture"—referring to a rigorous and critical approach—with "technology:"

The task of the educator I am convinced can be quite simply specified as follows:

to encourage the student to believe in architecture and technology;

to encourage the student to be skeptical about architecture and technology;

and then to cause the student to manipulate with passion and intelligence, the subjects or objects of [their] conviction and doubt.[7]

[1] The course was centered around an early generative design program, *Topdown*, developed at UCLA by William Mitchell and Robin Liggett. See Malcolm McCullough, "20 Years of Scripted Space," *Architectural Design* 76, no. 4 (July-August 2006), 12-15.

[2] Ibid., p. 14.

[3] See Alexander Caragonne, *The Texas Rangers: Notes from the Architectural Underground* (Cambridge, MA: MIT Press, 1995), "The Genesis."

[4] G. Shape Stiny, *Talking about Seeing and Doing* (Cambridge, MA: MIT Press, 2006).

[5] Joan Ockman, "The Road Not Taken," in *Autonomy and Ideology: Positioning an Avant-garde in America* (New York: Monacelli Press, 1997), 82.

[6] Peter Cook, *Drawing: The Motive Force of Architecture* (New York: Wiley, 2008), 135.

[7] Colin Rowe, "Architectural Education in the USA," *Lotus International* 24 (1980), 43.

"Hamstering," or the Joys and Uses of Architectural History

Christopher Long, Professor, Distinguished Teaching Professor. Faculty member since 1996.

IT IS, PERHAPS, an unlikely simile, but we historians are like hamsters. We collect materials and ideas—most of us obsessively—and store them away, safeguarding them for posterity, and, when need and occasion arise, "chew" on them later. For what historians do—and I find myself repeating this incessantly to my students—is to preserve memory and make meaning out of it.

My own "hamstering" often takes the form of searching through booksellers' catalogues for rare or unusual books, manuscripts, or photographs. Mostly, this bears little fruit. But, every once in a while, I stumble upon something wonderful. A few weeks past, I ordered a book from a vendor in Glen Cove, New York, a study on merchandising in the United States in the years before and after World War I. It wasn't a scarce work. It dealt with a subject I'm thinking about writing a book on: how the modernists of those years sought to transform public taste and to encourage consumers to buy their designs.

When the book arrived, included in the package was a supplemental catalogue from the same shop listing other items for sale. I poured over it. In the first several pages, I saw nothing particularly interesting. But, suddenly, my eyes caught an intriguing entry, a listing for a portfolio of twenty original photographs. The description was vague. It mentioned something about images of a war-damaged city—Berlin or Linz, the owner of the shop wasn't sure which—and efforts

Karl Schaechterle and Friedrich Tamms, Niebelungen Bridge, Linz, Austria, 1938-40;
view of the bridge under construction, c. 1939

to rebuild one of its bridges. Not much to go on. But the entry also listed the name of the photographer, one R. Stenzel Presse Photos, of Linz.

I doubted immediately that the photos were of Berlin. Why would a photographer in Linz be making photographs of war-torn Berlin? During World War II, much of the transportation network in Central Europe was destroyed, and it made no sense that someone from a smallish provincial city in Austria had undertaken what would have been an arduous journey to Berlin to document the reconstruction. I thought the images must be of Linz.

The advertisement also listed possible dates—the 1930s or 1940s. If the photos, of course, were actually from the 1930s, they would not have shown war damage, but, rather, urban renewal. The mention of a bridge also piqued my interest. Most all of the bridges spanning the Danube, which bisects Linz, were destroyed during the war. The photographs, I thought, might simply document the postwar reconstruction effort. On the other hand, if they were from the prewar period, I knew they might

be something else entirely. I recalled that in the late 1930s, Adolf Hitler, who had grown up in Linz, had taken a personal interest in redesigning the city. As an adolescent, he had been obsessed with architecture and urban planning, and he had spent hours sketching and re-sketching plans to rebuild the town on a monumental scale. His boyhood friend, August Kubizek, recalled that the first time he went to visit the fifteen-year-old Hitler in his home he found "his room littered with sketches, drawings, blueprints. Here was 'the new theatre,' there was the mountain hotel in the Lichtenberg—it was like an architect's office."[1] Later, when he came to power, Hitler returned to the idea of making the city "a second Budapest." In the 1930s, he also expended much time and energy on a plan to remake Berlin, enlisting the young Albert Speer to draw up a scheme. The redevelopment of Linz was left to another architect, a man named Hermann Giesler. I knew that Giesler had made extensive models and drawings of his ideas for the development of the waterfront in Linz. I wondered if the bridge mentioned in the catalogue was part of this rebuilding effort.

If the photographs were in fact of this project, I thought they might be rare. I couldn't recall having seen images of it, and, to confirm my hunch, reached for a book in my study, a huge tome—over a thousand pages—written by one of my old friends in Vienna, Helmut Weihsmann, on the history of Nazi architecture. There was a twenty-page single-spaced description of "Hitler's Linz" (Helmut is nothing if not thorough!), which included a section on the bridge—the so-called Nibelungen Bridge, after the German epic saga, the Niebelungenlied (Hitler had named the bridge himself)—and a photograph of the model of the entire project, but no other illustrations of it.[2] I began to wonder if I wasn't on to something.

I've never been especially interested in Nazi architecture; I write about modernism in the period before Hitler's rise to power. Nonetheless, the description in the catalogue continued to provoke my interest. What if these were indeed photographs of the bridge project? And twenty photos—a more or less complete document of it? The price listed for the whole album was $170. I had just received my annual royalty check from Yale University Press (royalty checks from academic presses are famously anemic—usually just about enough for a nice dinner or two out) and thought, "what the heck, money in, money out," and ordered the album.

The package arrived about a week and a half later. I opened it, and seeing the first image confirmed what I had suspected. The photographs were of Linz—not a war-damaged Linz, but the city as it had been before the allied bombing—and the images were of the new Nazi-era bridge. I flipped through the twenty plates, and what I saw was a very good set of photographs of the planning, preparation, and construction of the bridge and its surroundings. Now I was genuinely interested. I made a quick search of the project online and discovered that the bridge was the only one of Hitler's projects for Linz that was actually completed. It turned out that it was not Giesler's design but was instead the work of engineer Karl Schaechterle and architect Friedrich Tamms. Construction had begun in the late summer of 1938, not long after Germany annexed Austria, and was completed in 1940. The bridge survived the war and was captured by American troops in early May 1945.

I wanted to spend more time with the search, but I glanced at my watch and realized it was time for me to teach. I gathered up the pages of the portfolio and took it with me. It was a Monday morning, and the class was a seminar focused on Adolf Loos and Ludwig Mies van der Rohe, two of the seminal figures working in Central Europe on the eve of the war—not quite a match for this material, though close. But I thought this was a teachable moment, and when class began, I showed the students—a mixture of advanced undergrads and graduate students—the photographs and talked about what I suspected was their import.

Like almost all the history classes in the School of Architecture, the students in the seminar came from several programs. Most were budding designers, working toward their BArch or MArch degrees. Some also were from architectural history and historic preservation. What I wanted to convey to them in that moment was the joy of discovery, the thrill of finding something new about the past and trying to work out what it might mean. Those lessons are most immediate for the handful of our students who intend to go on and become professional historians. Yet the real delight I find in teaching in an architecture school is the challenge of how to make the past come alive for students who will not be historians. Even more pressing—and important—is the problem of how to make history relevant to them, a group whose preoccupations are with the present, of making and renewing our built environment. That question is always with me when I am in the classroom; it is a persistent, even hectoring, presence in my thoughts, a houseguest of my mind who has moved in and gives absolutely no indication of departing.

But what relevance does this bridge for Hitler have for the students of today? It is not a particularly affective

Karl Schaechterle and Friedrich Tamms, Niebelungen Bridge, Linz, 1938-40; model showing the bridge and two new adjacent buildings framing the entry to the city's main square

or lovely design. It's not like the Swiss designer Robert Maillart's elegant attenuated ribbons of concrete or Santiago Calatrava's poetic essays in structural form; it is actually rather dumpy, with some clunky statues and little else to recommend it. The association with Hitler, is, of course, meaningful in some way, especially for political and cultural historians. But can it tell us anything about design for today? That was the question I put to my students.

We chatted for a little while. I didn't want to spend too much time on it because we had other questions to address that day. It came to me, while one of the students was talking, that perhaps the best question lay not with the design itself or the circumstances of its making, but simply whether it was possible for a dictatorship—and not an especially enlightened one, to say the least—to produce an architecture that was suitable to its place and appropriate to its use. In other words, could Nazis make good architecture? Looking at what was built during the Nazi era, it is difficult to divorce the buildings from their makers, and it is easy to come to the determination that the great majority of what was put up in this time was pedestrian at best.

Still, as I stared at the photos of the bridge project before me, I thought: "it's really not so bad. It makes sense, and one can readily understand what Schaechterle and Tamms—at Hitler's behest—were trying to accomplish." Perhaps, I said to the class, one possible route to understanding would be to evaluate the rebuilding plan merely on its merits, seeing its flaws and faults, but also its response to place and function.

The students stared at the photos for a moment, and a number voiced their approval: "Yes, perhaps that might reveal something; it might be a way of seeing some value." It did not really matter to me that they agreed. Far more powerful and satisfying was that they were thinking historically. They had engaged the past, and, in that moment, they were searching for deeper truths.

[1]August Kubizek, *The Young Hitler I Knew*, trans. Geoffrey Brooks (London: Greenhill Books, 2006), 96.

[2]Helmuth Weihsmann, *Bauen unterm Hackenkreuz: Architektur des Untergangs* (Vienna: Promedia, 1998), 942-962.

Architectural History at the School of Architecture

MID student Elise King (MA '10) and PhD student Sam Dodd (MA '09) in the Alexander Architectural Archive

Architectural history has been a part of the school's professional curriculum from its earliest years. During the Beaux-Arts era before World War II, students were introduced to ancient Greek and Roman architecture by William J. Battle, professor of classics and long-standing chairman of the Faculty Building Committee. Architectural history took on a more critical edge in the 1950s through the teaching of Colin Rowe (1954-57) and Blake Alexander (1955-94). Alexander played a formative role in the historic preservation program and took a strong interest in the history of the campus, which was shared by Roxanne Williamson (1972-97). Anthony Alofsin joined the faculty in 1987 and established the PhD program. Today, alongside Alofsin, professors Miroslava Beneš, Richard Cleary, Michael Holleran, Fernando Lara,

Christopher Long, and Danilo Udovicki-Selb introduce students to and direct advanced work in the histories of architecture, landscape architecture, and urban design. In addition, other members of the school's faculty offer courses on topics of special interest. The candidates and graduates of the PhD program contribute to the field through publications addressing a range of topics in nineteenth-century American architecture and modernism in American and European architecture. The program's first dissertations have been published as books: William Owen Harrod, *Bruno Paul: The Life and Work of a Pragmatic Modernist* (2005); and Kathryn E. Holliday, *Leopold Eidlitz: Architecture and Idealism in the Gilded Age* (2008).

Diversity

The vision for the School of Architecture in the twenty-first century is for it to be a place that reflects the demographic diversity of Texas in terms of race, gender, and economic background. The design professions need members who can draw on a wide range of life experiences and bring multiple points of view to the challenges of shaping the built environment. While it is easy to agree with these sentiments, they are remarkably difficult to realize. Like architecture schools across the country, the UTSOA struggles to achieve the diversity among faculty and students to which it aspires.

In 2008, the school had 75 faculty members (permanent and adjunct) of which 49 were men and 26 were women. Sixty-eight of the group were classified as white. Among the 658 undergraduate and graduate students, 464 were classified as white, 3 as American Indian, 15 as African American, 51 as Asian American, 63 as Hispanic, and 70 were International Students. Overall, the ratio of women to men was about equal, however the distribution among programs is uneven. Interior design, landscape architecture, and historic preservation, for example, are strongly dominated by female populations.

The great legal victories that demolished the historic policies of racial discrimination in the 1950s were in some respects the easiest part of the problem to resolve, for while admission to the ranks of students, faculty, and registered professionals is now based on merit, the composition of candidate pools remains skewed. Many potential students from historically under-represented populations never learn that fields such as landscape architecture or planning exist or simply do not acquire the skills they need to qualify for undergraduate or graduate study at UT, despite their innate intelligence and aptitude. Many graduates, particularly women, do not earn professional registration (only 20 percent of licensed architects are women). Only a few schools prepare students to succeed in university teaching.

The issues reach far beyond the UTSOA, but the school is not helpless. It has a history that can be inspirational. From the beginning, enrollment has been open to women, an unusual circumstance in the early twentieth century. In 1950, the school's administration welcomed a pioneering African American student, John Saunders Chase, and in the late 1960s Dean Alan Taniguchi worked hard to increase the diversity of faculty and students. While more could have been done to build on these steps, we can look at them less in terms of opportunity lost than as deeds to emulate. In 2010, the school is launching a series of initiatives for increasing demographic diversity and ensuring that it fosters an open, enlightened, and robust learning environment.

Left: Chase enrolls at UT to pursue a master's degree in architecture, June 7, 1950

Below: Chase (MArch '52) and his wife, Drucie, in front of the San Antonio Garage at 25th and San Antonio streets, designed by Chase in 1994

JOHN SAUNDERS CHASE (MARCH '52), FAIA, was the first African American to graduate from the University of Texas. He earned a BS in Architecture from Hampton University in 1948 and later moved to Austin to work for the Lott Lumber Company. Less than a year after his arrival in Austin, Chase heard about the Sweatt v. Painter case pending before the U.S. Supreme Court that challenged the university's exclusion of black students from the Law School. Recognizing the broader implications of the case, Chase contacted Architecture Chairman Hugh McMath, who encouraged him to apply to the school and await the outcome. When the court overturned the university's policy in 1950, Chase was among the first African Americans to enroll in the graduate and professional schools. (African Americans would not be permitted to enroll in undergraduate programs until the Supreme Court's Brown v. Board of Education in 1954.)

Following his graduation from the UTSOA, Chase became the first African American licensed to practice architecture in Texas and the first African American to be admitted to the Texas Society of Architects and the American Institute of Architects chapter in Houston, where he has based his practice. Over his long and distinguished career, Chase has designed a wide range of buildings and has devoted much time and energy to professional and public service. The AIA named him a Fellow in 1990 and UT awarded him its Distinguished Alumni Award in 1992. Part of Chase's legacy is the National Organization of Minority Architects, for which he was a founding member in 1971. The UTSOA currently has an active chapter.

Above: Students working in the drafting room of the Engineering Building, before 1927

Right: Alpha Alpha Gamma, women's honorary and professional fraternity, 1947

It would seem that women are particularly fitted for the profession of an architect, especially in the work of design and in the appreciation of decorative possibilities in building.

-Dallas Morning News, 1910

Women have been part of the school from its inception, and the early faculty encouraged their enrollment. In 1912, philanthropist George Washington Brackenridge established a scholarship fund for female architecture students. Of the four students in the graduating class of 1915, two were women. When Alpha Alpha Gamma, a women's honorary and professional fraternity, was established nationally in 1922, a chapter was founded at UT. Members attended national conventions and met locally to advance issues regarding women in architectural practice. Despite their visibility in the school, however, many women did not complete their degrees in architecture.

During the two world wars, the percentage of women in the school rose sharply as men were called away to military service. The influx of veterans after the wars swelled class sizes and overwhelmed facilities. Following World War II, women were actively discouraged from studying architecture. The papers of Ida C. Scott (attended 1944-77) in the Alexander

Architectural Archive offer rich insights into the educational and career opportunities for women attending the school at this time. Once the veterans graduated, female enrollment gradually increased, but women composed only 10% of graduates from the 1950s through the 1970s. That situation has changed. By the 1990s, over 40% of architecture students in the school were female, and, in the 2009-10 academic year, women accounted for 56% of the bachelors degree recipients.

FACULTY PIONEERS

Professor Emeritus Gerlinde Leiding joined the faculty in 1968 with an undergraduate degree in architecture from Werkkustschule Krefeld in Germany and a MArch from Yale. In 1972 she became the school's first tenured female professor. A gifted studio instructor, she also taught courses in Asian architecture and created a study abroad program in Japan. She received the Texas Excellence Teaching Award in 1990. Her research interests addressed vernacular architecture in Japan and Texas. She retired in 2007.

Natalie de Blois was an accomplished architect when she came to teach her first design studio at UT in 1980. Working her way through the ranks, she was the first woman to be named senior designer at Skidmore, Owings & Merrill, and participated in designing many of the firm's iconic mid-century skyscrapers including Lever House (as assistant to Gordon Bunshaft), and the Pepsi Cola and Union Carbide buildings (as senior architect). De Blois remained an adjunct professor until 1993, teaching Advanced Architectural Design, Visual Communication, and Technical Communication. For her students, these rigorous studios were a rite of passage.

Sandra Rosenbloom joined the faculty as assistant professor in 1972. A decade later she became the first woman to attain the rank of professor (1982) and was named the David Bruton, Jr. Centennial Professor of Urban Design and Planning. In 1990, she left UT to become director of the Drachman Institute of for Land and Regional Development Studies at the University of Arizona. She is an internationally recognized scholar whose work explores the intersection of the social sciences and transportation through topics such as the transportation needs of women and the elderly.

Being a woman architect is not the important thing to me. I've always been singled out because I'm the one who did large buildings, but architecture is a building profession.

-Natalie de Blois

Left: Natalie de Blois examining a skyscraper model with her students, 1980s

Bottom Left: Sandra Rosenbloom, 1989

Bottom Right: Gerlinde Leiding, ca. 1990

You've Come a Long Way, Baby—
Women and the Profession of
Interior Design at The University of Texas

Nancy Kwallek, Gene Edward Mikeska Endowed Chair in Interior Design.
Faculty member since 1983.

Some leaders are born women.

—Geraldine Ferraro

Throughout the young history of interior design, there has been a select group of women whose style and impact made others around them indistinct by comparison. The women responsible for the establishment of the discipline cannot be classified as "ordinary." They engaged in design within their respective times and drew attention to meanings which enhance our understanding of the relationship of women with the designed interior environment. Two such women in particular were Elsie de Wolfe (1865-1950) and Dorothy Draper (1889-1969). However, now that our reading of the history of design and decoration is more fine-tuned, we can identify other strong women in the discipline and on its fringes who laid the foundation for where we are today. Though less well known than de Wolfe and Draper, they helped establish the groundwork for the field of interior design at the University of Texas. Looking back at these pioneering women, themes arise that can inform the ways in which we might approach the discipline in the future.

The Beginning of the Interior Design Program at UT

Mary Edna Gearing (1872-1946)
UT's First Female Full Professor and Administrator

Left to right: Ellen Swallow Richards, Mary Edna Gearing, Anna Brightman

Born in Pittsburgh, Pennsylvania, Mary Edna Gearing's family moved to Texas when she was young. She graduated from high school in Houston in 1888 and beyond high school received a liberal education from private tutors with a focus on economics. Miss Gearing was a moving force among a small group of educators who met yearly at Lake Placid, New York, between 1902 and 1909 to discuss women's education and ways to improve the standards for a quality life. The leader of the Lake Placid Conferences was Ellen Swallow Richards (1842-1911) who founded "the science of better living" movement and in 1908 organized the yearly conferences on "human ecology."[1] The art of living was an integral part of Richards' philosophy. Richards had a significant influence on Miss Gearing. Both believed that the "quality of life depends upon the ability of society to teach its members how to live in harmony with their environment—defined first as family, then as community, then as the world and its resources."[2]

After heading the domestic arts department at New York University, Miss Gearing came to UT in 1912—only one year after the completion of Battle Hall—and began a similar program in domestic arts at the request of President Sidney Edward Mezes. She was the first woman to hold the ranks of professor and department chair and the first female administrator in the history of the University of Texas System.

Although Miss Gearing's area of expertise was economics,

she was also interested in the decorative arts and had a strong pioneering spirit to bring her ideas to fruition.[3] At UT, one of her major interests was in connection with the university building program. From 1925 to 1937, she was a member of the Faculty Building Committee, where she set standards for the furnishing of spaces on campus.

The former Home Economics building at the intersection of 24th Street and Inner Campus Drive, which she planned in conjunction with campus architect Paul Cret, was built in 1933. It was renamed in her honor in 1976. Its original interior, portions of which remain, is a testament to her forcefulness in creating a learning environment that reflected her fine taste and artistic ability. Working with Cret, she installed a variety of different finishes and surface treatments for study purposes, so the students could learn how to create a unified whole.

As a tribute to the pioneering spirit of Texas women, Miss Gearing had four areas of the building depict different eras of home life in Texas history. The Great Hall—the central lobby—contained exhibits typical of the various nationalities who settled in the state. Opening off the Great Hall, the Pioneer Room, with fireplace and wrought iron implements, represented the modest households of pioneer days. Also on the first floor, a Plantation Bedroom was furnished with a four-poster bed and symbols of the Old South. On the third floor, still extant, is a parlor and dining room, designed and decorated according to Miss Gearing's wishes, in keeping with the traditions during the days of the Republic of Texas. The president of the American Institute of Designers and friend of the department was commissioned to turn the suite into a family home setting typical of the Republic of Texas. Most of the furniture belonged originally to pioneer Texas families and was later given to the university. Miss Gearing used her own money to buy a mahogany Empire dining table and Grecian-style curved-back chairs for the dining room from Marshall Fields in Chicago to complete the space.

The first course in interior design was taught in 1927 during Miss Gearing's leadership. By the time she retired in 1942, after thirty-one years as chairwoman, the home economics department was offering six majors including an emphasis area in interior design. In 1945, it established the first interior design program west of the Mississippi.

Dr. Anna Brightman (1921-1990)
A Beacon of Leadership

The major force in the development of the new program was Dr. Anna Brightman, who joined the faculty in 1946 as professor and Head of the Division of Interior Design. During her professorship, she taught courses on historic furniture and the decorative arts and conducted research on historic American furnishings.

In 1952, Brightman was joined by a male colleague, Dr. Charles York, and, together, they spent the next few decades

Parlor of the Republic Suite, Mary E. Gearing Hall, University of Texas at Austin

establishing the division's strong professional foundation. For many years—up until the late 1980s—interior design students took their foundation courses in basic design and visual communication in the School of Architecture.[4] This underscored the link between interior design and architecture, as the disciplines were beginning to practice together in the profession.

Dr. Brightman was a founding member of the Interior Design Educators Council (commonly referred to today as IDEC), a professional organization for interior design educators nationwide. She was also a founding member of the Foundation of Interior Design Education Research (FIDER, now renamed as the Council for Interior Design Accreditation, CIDA), the international accrediting agency for interior design programs. Her work in these two associations helped to give positive notice to the University of Texas as having one of the finest interior design programs in the country. Under her leadership, the program was accredited by FIDER in 1973, shortly after its founding, making it one of the first five programs in the nation to earn such designation.

Continued Excellence and
the Move to the School of Architecture

Dr. Brightman's contributions to the designing of interiors paved the way for a whole generation of Texas designers. After serving as head of the Interior Design Division for thirty-five years, she went on leave in 1981 and retired two years later. Charles York briefly assumed the head position from 1981 to 1983. He retired in 1985 and passed away in 2004. After Dr. York stepped down from the leadership position in 1983, I became the Head of the Division of Interior Design in the Department of Human Ecology.[5]

Following a successful re-accreditation review in 1994, former provost Mark Yudof asked me and Dean Lawrence Speck for our views about moving the program to the School of Architecture. We both agreed that the school was a more suitable home for interior design and immediately began working on a smooth transition. In 1997, the Interior Design program was officially moved from the College of Natural Sciences, Department of Human Ecology, to the School of Architecture, adding a fourth professional degree to the school alongside those in architecture (BArch and MArch) and community and regional planning (MSCRP). The move meant student admission requirements in the new program would be much more stringent because of long standing architecture accreditation requirements of dedicated studio space for each student in design. The increased selectivity has raised the program's standard of excellence.

The Program Today

Since the inception of the interior design option sixty-five years ago, the program has achieved many accomplishments that few others in the country have attained. We probably are unique in our endowments that foster excellence, including an endowed chair, a centennial lectureship, two endowed lecture series, and, for students, an endowed presidential scholarship and an endowed third-year scholarship. Such support has allowed the program to consistently rank among the top interior design programs in the nation. Our students have been frequent recipients of the largest and most prestigious national interior design student competition, the Angelo Donghia Interior Design Senior Scholarship. Since its inception in 2003, seven of our students have been awarded the scholarship, totaling approximately $210,000, that provides each student $30,000 for the final year of study.

To further strengthen and bring recognition to our program, we now offer a master of interior design (MID) degree. The MID will help advance the technical and theoretical development of the discipline and allow students to pursue significant questions in the material, methods, theory, and performance factors in interior environments. MID students will also be encouraged to research critical social, professional and technical aspects of sustainable design and the health and well-being of human populations. As the slogan goes: "You've come a long way, baby!"

---

[1] Ellen Swallow Richards was the first woman admitted to MIT; many institutions turned her down on the basis of her gender, and MIT accepted her as a special student to ascertain women's ability in the sciences. As far back as 1892, she promoted the idea of sustainability. As a Trustee for Vassar College, she advised the college to construct an irrigation plant instead of building a sewage canal to the Hudson River. Her interest in the environment led her to introduce the term "ecology" into the English language. She developed the study of "human ecology" (home economics) and the Summer Institute of Euthenics—the center for studies in families, child psychology, child nutrition, and methods of education—ultimately including faculty members Benjamin Spock and Margaret Mead. http://vcencyclopedia.vassar.edu/alumni/ellen-swallow-richards.html

[2] See http://vcencyclopedia.vassar.edu/alumni/ellen-swallow-richards.html

[3] For Gearing's strength as a force within the state of Texas and the nation, see Judith N. McArthur, *Creating the New Woman: The Rise of Southern Women's Progressive Culture in Texas, 1893-1918* (Urbana: University of Illinois Press, 1998); and see Lucy Rathbone, "Mary E. Gearing, Pioneer," *Journal of Home Economics* 39 (January 1947); "Texas Women: A Celebration of History," Archives, Texas Woman's University, Denton; Vertical Files, Dolph Briscoe Center for American History, University of Texas at Austin.

[4] Students could choose to take their four foundation design and visual communication courses from either the School of Architecture or the College of Fine Arts; most of them chose the School of Architecture route.

[5] In 1990 the name of the department was changed from Home Economics to Human Ecology in recognition of the true meaning of the discipline as established by Ellen Swallow Richards.

Practitioners + Academics:
A Team-Teaching Approach
to Interior Design Studios

Carl Matthews, Associate Professor. Faculty member since 2003.
Caroline Hill, Assistant Professor, Texas State University–San Marcos

THERE IS A COMMON JOKE among people outside of academia that "those who can—do; those who can't—teach." In reality, teaching in practice-based disciplines like architecture and interior design requires faculty who can both "do" and "teach." Traditionally, programs have hired at least some studio faculty with strong professional practice backgrounds to bridge gaps between academia and practice. In this scenario, design faculty would ideally be completely engaged in their scholarly and teaching duties while simultaneously plugged into practice. However, the rigors of academia do not always allow for this duality. Referencing this link between academia and practice, Boyer and Mitgang state:

The worlds of architecture practice and education depend on each other for their purpose and vitality. Both bear responsibility for preparing students for gainful employment and for continuing the lifelong professional education of architects. In the end, the academy and the profession also share an obligation to serve the needs of communities, the built environment, and society as a whole. It is inconceivable that these goals can ever be effectively realized in an atmosphere clouded by miscommunication, mistrust, or lack of respect.[1]

While this statement speaks to the discipline of architecture, it is just as relevant to interior design (ID). Over the years, studio faculties have found a variety of ways to acknowledge this truth and successfully bridge

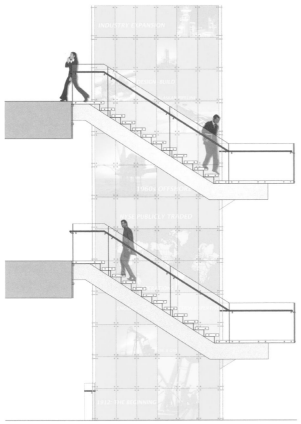

Saskia Fazio, Lydia Mason, and Garrett Seaman; Fluor Headquarters, Dallas, TX: Advanced Design, Carl Matthews and Gensler (Dallas), critics, 2006

the gap between academia and practice while also respecting other curriculum goals, such as theory and research. One frequently used strategy for injecting a practice-based perspective into the equation is to invite practitioners to student critiques. One drawback to only inviting practitioners in for a brief interim or final critiques is that their engagement in the design process is too limited. In an effort to engage practitioners more directly in the day-to-day teaching component of the studio, the authors of this paper have implemented an alternative method of engaging practitioners in ID education.

Who? Liaisons to the School of Architecture

From 2002 to 2010, six design firms volunteered to team-teach fourteen interior design studios. Strong ties to alumni provided direct links to practitioners eager to participate in the team-teaching model. Gensler's Dallas office was the first partnering firm. Judy Pesek (BS '78), Partner in Charge of the office was particularly interested in students getting a full understanding of the design process from marketing through construction documentation. Wilson Associates (Dallas) became the

second partnering firm in 2003. President Trisha Wilson (BS '69) was interested in students experiencing the wide variety of challenges that large-scale hospitality design requires. From 2004 through 2008, the Fall Advanced Design Studio alternated between partnering with Gensler and Wilson Associates. The studios were interdisciplinary, including fourth-year interior design students, fourth-year architecture students, and graduate architecture students. In 2009, graduate historic preservation students were added, and Overland Partners (San Antonio), a firm with a rich portfolio of preservation-oriented projects, was engaged as the partnering firm.

After the first three years of working with Gensler and Wilson, the Austin-based firm STG Design expressed appreciation for the team-teaching model and requested to participate in a similar way. This enabled ID faculty during the third-year spring semesters from 2005 through 2008 to integrate the team-teaching model. For these studios, the faculty and practitioners selected current or recently completed contracts in the STG office that would support curricular objectives. In spring 2009, Beck Group (Dallas) was the partnering firm and in Spring 2010, RTKL (Dallas) chose to participate.

It is interesting to note that practitioners donating most of their time in recent years have been alumni who participated in some of the earliest partnerships

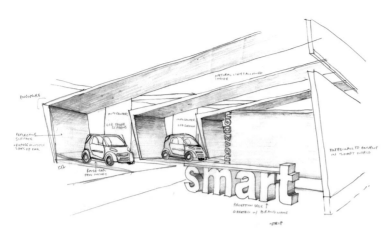

Brittany Cooper, Smart Car Dealership, Austin, TX: Design VI Interiors, Carl Matthews and STG Design (Austin), critics, 2008

as students. Now, not only are we seeing graduates sustain successful careers in practice, but we are also seeing a desire in our students-turned-practitioners to "give back" to the UT program.

What? The Details of the Team Taught Studio

At the beginning of the semester, faculty members worked collaboratively with practitioners to define the project type and scope to meet curriculum goals and accreditation standards, and practitioners were given design authority equal to the faculty member in the studio. Faculty, however, were solely responsible for final grade assignments.

Projects integrated theoretical components and academic research into the design process. For example, student discussions were supplemented with scholarly articles relative to project type, and students undertook independent research. This balance of practice and theory resulted in improved quality of student work and met curriculum objectives.

During the fall semesters 2002-2004, design firms team-taught design studios with one faculty coordinator. Practitioners from the firms teamed with the professor and co-taught the studio two times per week. Assignments were based on actual projects the firms had completed, and students presented their work to clients and other firm members and toured the completed projects at the end of the semester. The structure and requirements of the studios varied to capitalize on the firm's expertise and interests in differing design market sectors. Based on feedback from students, colleagues, and practitioners, it was determined that twice-a-week practitioner presence throughout the semester was too much. In subsequent

years (2005-2009), practitioners met with students approximately seven to sixteen times throughout the semester. These meetings took the form of informal desk critiques, formal presentations, and teaching of specialized information.

Although the majority of student-practitioner interactions took place face-to-face in the studio, there were some variations to this scenario. For example, in some instances, the students traveled to the firm headquarters to present their final projects (e.g. Dallas). In another semester, when partnering with RTKL, also headquartered in Dallas, some interactions occurred via e-mail and follow-up conference calls. The thoughtful use of technology tools in support of the team-teaching process (e-mail, telephone conferencing, and video conferencing) opens the door to even more opportunities for engaging practitioners from firms outside the university's immediate geographical area.

In the spirit of sharing knowledge to advance the profession, we presented our success with the team-teaching model at the 2010 Interior Design Educator's Council National Conference where it generated considerable interest from other design programs. Closer to home, it has been successfully adapted to the interior design program at Texas State University-San Marcos.

Summary

The practitioner-academic studio model engages practitioners in design education beyond their commonly assigned role of project critic. Based on the experiences of the faculty involved, this type of collaboration can be a win-win for all parties involved.   The team-taught ID studios enhanced the educational outcomes for students and resulted in mutually beneficial experiences for the faculty and professional practitioners. According to Gensler's Judy Pesek, her staff members beg to volunteer, because the experience of mentoring the students is exciting and brings fresh ideas into the office.

In addition to energizing the practitioners, the collaborations have helped faculty keep abreast of changes in the industry. Prior to experiencing the team-teaching model, we found it necessary to return to interior design practice during the summer months in order to update our knowledge and remain current in interior design issues. Since engaging the team-teaching model, the need to return to practice has diminished because the partnering firms bring in new challenges and information on a weekly basis throughout the school year. Additionally, the firms bring specialized information in areas such as historic preservation or medical design into the curriculum, which broadens the studio experience.

While the workload can be intense, student evaluations for the courses are consistently high, and the quality of the work produced is excellent. In the third-year course at the School of Architecture, instructor evaluation scores improved by an average of 22.5 percent and overall course evaluation scores improved by an average of 9.5 percent. Students consistently wrote positive statements about the course content and structure on evaluations. The presence of another teacher in the studio classroom also encourages students to explore a greater range of ideas, promotes discussions of practice-related topics that don't generally enter a purely academic studio, and allows for inspiring field trips to firm offices and completed projects.

Practitioners from other (non-partnering) firms frequently compliment the quality of work seen in student portfolios and note the students' improved verbal presentation skills. Both programs (UT and Texas State) have had very positive accreditation reviews since the team-teaching strategy was implemented. The process also led to more creative solutions and a more rigorous studio climate. Since 2005, six students have used projects from the studios to win the prestigious Donghia scholarship in addition to other scholarships.

The practitioner-academic strategy responds to the Boyer report's call to the academy and the profession to jointly accept responsibility for preparing students to address the future.

Sarah Jean Ellis, Jennifer Lee, and Sarah Wistner; Starr Building, Austin, TX: Advanced Design, Carl Matthews and Overland Partners (San Antonio), 2009

The authors thank the following participating firms for their contribution and dedication to this effort: Gensler, Wilson Associates, STG Design, Beck Group, Carson Design Associates, Overland Partners, and RTKL.

[1] E. L. Boyer and L.D. Mitgang, *Building Communities: A New Future for Architecture Education and Practice* (Princeton, New Jersey: The Carnegie Foundation for the Advancement of Teaching, 1996), 107.

A Visit to the Interior Design Studio

Lois Weinthal, Associate Professor. Faculty member since 2009.

AS THE SCHOOL of architecture celebrates 100 years, the interior design program recently passed its first decade within the school and is looking towards its second. During this time, the program has consistently ranked in the top ten nationally (but who's keeping track?). We have had students expand the boundary of the curriculum by traveling abroad, seeking internships, and winning the prestigious $30,000 national Donghia Award in consecutive years. Not just one student per year, but two!

The program is small in number—one studio section per year—but visible due to the work the students produce. The work itself has changed over the years with faculty members who have brought a range of influences, from those who tackle alternative studio programs like the design of airplane interiors to one who led the school's Solar Decathlon team. My teaching within the program has allowed me to integrate my interests in full-scale construction, whether at the scale of clothing, furniture, or architectural interiors, in the undergraduate Interior Design V studio. Students explore clothing as a measure of the body and textile as a measure of the interior. They apply their findings to the scale of furniture, whereby they step up the scale of materials and tools as they learn how to bend plywood with a vacuum press and tap and drill steel to produce furniture forms that mimic the reclining body. The final review resembles a fashion show followed by reviewers testing out furniture. At

John Vehko,
Design Lab
supervisor, assists
students using
the vacuum press
to fabricate bent
plywood furniture:
Interior Design
V, Lois Weinthal,
critic, 2006

the Advanced Design level, I ask students to explore architectural interiors with full-scale constructions that turn the Jean & Bill Booziotis Loggia of Goldsmith Hall into a temporary exhibition space. My sense is that a bonding occurs amongst the students, or at least I know it does for me. We volunteer with Habitat for Humanity as an opportunity to become familiar with the weight of materials, and we transform the loggia into a mini-construction site with spotlights to allow for work at night. The studio spills out into the loggia, and the final review is a full engagement with the work.

The start of the 2010 fall semester brings even more visibility to the Interior Design program with the launch of the master of interior design degree. The inaugural class will set a new benchmark for graduate studies in interior design. The program builds upon the strengths of the school and the university as a whole by integrating courses from across campus as electives in the curriculum. Students will have the opportunity to reach into the Anthropology Department and take Household Archaeology (how cool is that!) or the Design Division of Fine Arts and take Design Persuasion (and we all know how important that is during final reviews). The curriculum reflects the larger agenda of the school with its emphasis on sustainability and asserting the importance of cultural awareness with a semester-study abroad. In the end, graduates from the program will bring innovative areas of knowledge to practice and academia.

The year 2010 brings change to the School of Architecture and specifically to the Interior Design program. I don't think I will be here to comment on the bicentennial, but I hope to be here to reflect upon the master's program after its first decade.

Time for a Change:
Interior Design or Interior Architecture?

Nancy Kwallek, Gene Edward Mikeska Endowed Chair in Interior Design.
Faculty member since 1983.

To improve is to change;
to be perfect is to change often

-Winston Churchill

In the beginning decades of the twentieth century, women, such as Mary Edna Gearing, the first female administrator in the University of Texas System, indirectly or directly helped establish the profession of designing interior spaces, known then as interior decoration. However, in 1937, the College of Engineering, which then included the Department of Architecture, published a bulletin titled, "'OPPORTUNITIES'—Engineering and Architecture," wherein architecture was defined as a profession with "the blending of the arts and the sciences."[1] The bulletin describes the specialty areas within architecture and identifies a course in Interior Architecture, offered "for students who prefer the design, decoration, and furnishings of interiors." It goes on to say, "In practice they are often known as Interior Decorators, which is an inadequate title." Seventy-three years later, the point is even more compelling in light of the training and education that our interior design students receive in the School of Architecture. The time may have finally come to change the name of our discipline from interior design to interior architecture. Let us look at some arguments.

When comparing our program with the definitions, taxonomy of programs, and Classification of Instructional Programs (CIPs) developed by the U.S. Department of Education's National Center for Education, there is a strong argument for change. First, the U.S. Department of Education, Institute of Education Sciences (IES) defines Interior Design as:

An instructional program in the applied visual arts that prepares individuals to apply artistic principles and techniques to the professional planning, designing, equipping, and furnishing of residential and commercial interior spaces. [It] includes instruction in drafting and graphic techniques; principles of interior lighting, acoustics, systems integration, and color coordination; furniture and furnishings; textiles and their finishing; the history of interior design and period styles; basic structural design; building codes and inspection regulations; and applications to office, hotel, factory, restaurant and housing design.[2]

Figure 1 illustrates a mock-up sample board created in 1956 by Florence Knoll Bassett that illustrates colors, furniture, and textures for one of her clients. She is given credit as the first designer and architect to use such a technique, which has become the mainstay for interior design programs across the country. However, our program goes quite beyond representing the finished selection of materials.

In contrast, this definition of Interior Architecture by the IES more appropriately applies to our program:

An instructional program that prepares individuals for the independent professional practice of interior architecture— the processes and techniques of designing living, work and leisure indoor environments as integral components of a building system. [It] includes instruction in building design and structural systems, heating and cooling systems, safety and health standards, and interior design principles and standards.[3]

Figures 2 and 3 illustrate visual presentations for coursework generated from our program where students are instructed to understand interior systems and structural elements of an interior. They are trained to understand and visually interpret design through study models, finished models, and renderings. These finished renderings exemplify the students' ability to illustrate their understanding in the third dimension.

In addition, another strong argument is when one considers how the IES situates these two titles and

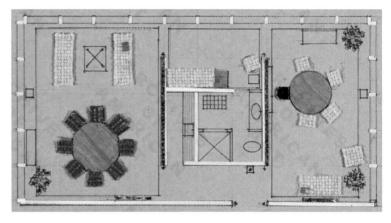

Fig. 1: Florence Knoll, sample board for Jack Heinz's office suite, Heinz Research Center, Pittsburgh, PA, 1956

descriptions within its taxonomy. On one hand, Interior Design resides under programs of the Visual and Performing Arts. Disciplines under this umbrella are described as those "programs that focus on the creation and interpretation of works and performances that use auditory, kinesthetic, and visual phenomena to express ideas and emotions in various forms, subject to aesthetic criteria." On the other hand, the description for programs under Architecture and Related Services, where Interior Architecture resides, describes those "programs that prepare individuals for professional practice in the various architecture-related fields and focus on the study of related aesthetic and socioeconomic aspects of the built environment." The educational goals of our curriculum and program align closely with this latter definition. Our program specifically addresses the socioeconomic aspects of design throughout the

Fig. 2: Kimberly Cole (BSID '10 and Angela Donghia Senior Scholarship recipient), interior architecture presentation

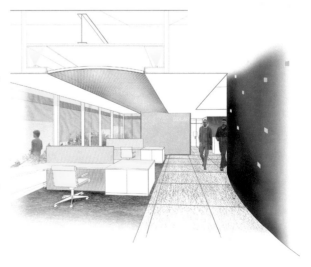

curriculum and, most specifically, through a particular required course: Designing for Human Behavior.

Though perhaps unintentional, the taxonomy of programs classified in CIPs establishes a hierarchy of importance or value to the public, which, in turn, affects the public's perception of academic programs and, thus, where parents' desires might rest in support of their children's pursuit of a major plan of study. CIP identifies programs in Architecture and Related Services as preparing individuals for professional practice. The classification also includes disciplines such as landscape architecture, urban design, community and regional planning, and architecture—all represented, with interior design, in the School of Architecture. On the other hand, the Visual and Performing Arts classification focuses on works that express ideas and emotions and includes many more unrelated disciples such as folk art, dance, and apparel design. These distinctions generally describe interior architecture as a profession and interior design as primarily focused on aesthetics and thus narrowing the academic breadth of a field that is inherently broad, rigorous, and interdisciplinary.

In other organizations and at websites for prospective students, interior design programs indicate that students will research styles and materials and choose finishes for interiors, while interior architecture programs indicate that students will study design history, build physical and virtual models, and learn building codes.[4] This distinction exacerbates the division in the design

community already facing challenges to its validity as a formal and rigorous discipline from external forces.

An external force making an impact on the profession in Texas is a law that has created a fuzzy boundary between registered and non-registered interior designers.[5] This has become a most pressing reason to consider the move toward the phrase, interior architecture, because our field is a distinctive profession grounded in education, research, accreditation, and licensure. The title of interior designer now does not require formal education or an examination—allowing individuals who have not earned a post-secondary degree in interior design from an accredited university to classify themselves as professional interior designers.

The name change is also important to increasing gender diversity. The term interior architecture, by its very nature, melds two traditionally gender-biased professions—interior design, which has been predominately female, to that of architecture, which has been predominately male. This is an invaluable advantage of pursuing a program that evolves to interior architecture—a name that both men and women would find more inviting and appropriate.

Based on these arguments, the current educational goals of our curriculum and program undoubtedly meet the definition of interior architecture much more accurately than that of interior design. As we move into the twenty-first century, it is important that we acknowledge that this persistent question—the current name of the program—does not fully represent the full scope of our discipline here at the University of Texas.

The development of the ability to think, analyze, and solve problems enables our students to pursue a professional life based on a sound educational foundation. Only those professionals able to analyze problems and solutions beyond the currently understood norms can be competent in adapting to social change, advancing technology, and growing legal pressures. Maybe it is time to go back full circle to the name that was originally suggested in 1937 by renaming our program and degree "Interior Architecture," a term attractive to international students because of its usage elsewhere in the world and, especially, to domestic students and parents who have reservations about the program because of their long-standing misconceptions about interior design.

[1] *The University of Texas Bulletin*, "'Opportunities'"—Engineering and Architecture" No. 3727, July 15, 1937, Alexander Architectural Archive, SoA, Box MMATH 1, file 13.

[2] See http://nces.ed.gov/pubs2002/cip2000/ciplist.asp?CIP2=50.

[3] http://nces.ed.gov/pubs2002/cip2000/ciplist90.asp?CIP2=04.

[4] See http://www.collegeboard.com/csearch/majors_careers/

[5] See Texas House Bill 1484, <http://www.legis.state.tx.us/BillLookup/Text.aspx?LegSess=81R&Bill=HB1484>, which amends state restrictions where now anyone may refer to him- or herself as an interior designer, while only a Texas Board of Architecture Examiners (TBAE) registrant may call him- or herself a "registered interior designer."

Planning and Urban Design

The relief efforts of the New Deal in the 1930s spurred nationwide interest in private homebuilding and public housing, which the war-related rebuilding plans of the 1940s and 1950s sustained. In response, the school initially drew on the planning expertise of Walter Rolfe. Armed with degrees from Kansas State and MIT, he had joined the faculty in 1924 and led the school from 1935 to 1946. He served on the Austin city planning commission from 1944 to 1946.

Hugo Leipziger's (later Leipziger-Pearce) appointment to the faculty in 1939 was transformative. A political refugee from Germany via France and Australia, Leipziger-Pearce had studied under Hans Poelzig at the Art Academy in Breslau and at the University of Hamburg and brought extensive professional experience with him to Austin. He developed a curriculum in community and regional planning and was a prolific scholar and practioner. Among his early publications is *The Architectonic City in America: Significant Origins, Forms, and Prospects* (UT Press, 1944).

The school initiated a five-year B.Arch in Regional and City Planning in 1944. The curriculum emphasized an interdisciplinary approach; students were encouraged to take courses in sociology, government, and economics. Studio projects addressed city and regional planning issues, including rehabilitation efforts for Texas towns and the redevelopment of Austin slums. Community and shopping centers became common design problems for students in the 1940s, predicting their cultural importance in the building boom of the postwar period. From this initiative grew the graduate programs in Community and Regional Planning, accredited by the American Institute of Planners in 1960, and Urban Design.

So far, little attention has been paid to subjects like physiology, psychology, biology, human and social geography, ecology, and regionalism, which have to make decisive contributions to the scheme of environmental planning...
          -Hugo Leipziger-Pearce, 1944.

Walter T. Rolfe, 1943

Leipziger-Pearce with Austin Mayor Lester Palmer discussing his plans for the Austin Central Business District, 1961

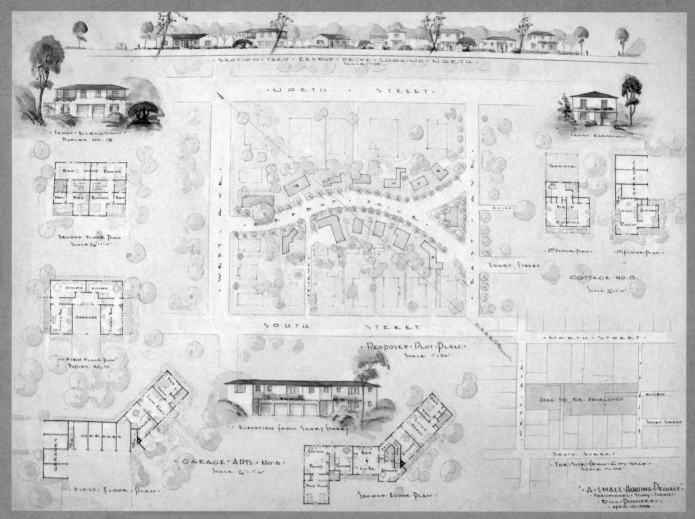

Bill Pounders (BArch '38), A Small Housing Project, 1938

EARLY COURSES ON HOUSING AND PLANNING:

DOMESTIC ARCHITECTURE:
First offered in the early 1930s and taught by Goldwin Goldsmith. The popular course offered "a study of residence design and the principles and problems of home planning." Goldsmith focused on many phases of homebuilding, including site selection and heating and ventilation.

PRINCIPLES OF HOUSING AND CITY PLANNING: First offered in 1941 by Leipziger-Pearce. "Designed primarily for students in sociology, government, economics, and architecture. Modern housing and city planning, their historical background, legal aspects, and elements of the physical and social development of the city, particularly with reference to Texas municipalities."

PROBLEMS OF HOUSING AND COMMUNITY PLANNING: First offered in 1943 by Leipziger-Pearce. "Integration and coordination of advanced knowledge and experimentation in the technical, social, and physical sciences with planning for housing, civic, and regional environment of modern communities."

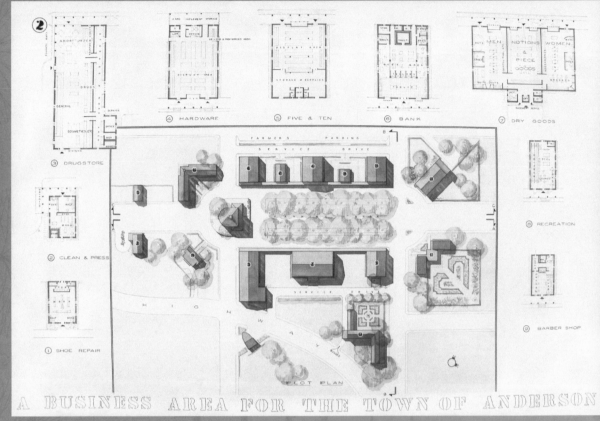

Right: Ernest Lewis Youens (BArch '41), A Business Area for the Town of Anderson, 1941

Bottom Left: A Neighborhood Unit, 1962

Bottom Right: Master Plan for Brady, Texas, 1960

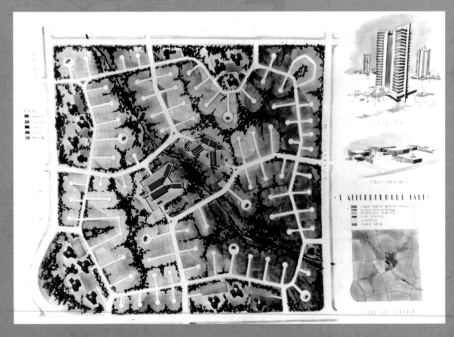

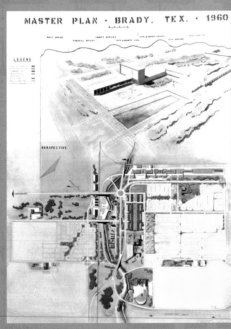

CRP TODAY

Since the arrival of Leipziger-Pearce, UT has offered interdisciplinary training in planning, with attention to sociological and economic, quantitative and qualitative approaches to the built environment. The CRP program today offers a MSCRP, a PhD, and opportunities for dual degrees with Urban Design, Sustainable Design, Latin American Studies, and Law. Students can tailor their education to focus on a specialization in Economic and Community Development, Environmental and Natural Resources Planning, Historic Preservation, Housing, Land Use and Land Development, or Transportation Planning.

Above: Dean Fritz Steiner maps options at a Community Forum held to solicit citizen input for Austin's new comprehensive plan, Filmore Middle School, 2010.

Left: Elementary school students in Santo Domingo, Dominican Republic, review the work of Bjørn Sletto's Applied Geographic Information Systems class, 2009

COURSES CURRENTLY OFFERED:

INTRODUCTION TO GIS (GEOGRAPHIC INFORMATION SYSTEMS): Taught by Bjørn Sletto. "Consists of two major components—the social dimensions of GIS and the techniques of GIS. The intent is to teach skills that will make you fluent in the uses of GIS, but also to help you understand the role that GIS, and you, as a GIS specialist, play in society."

QUALITATIVE METHODS FOR PLANNERS: Taught by Elizabeth Mueller. "Topics covered will include: designing a research strategy, writing good questions for interviews or surveys, conducting interviews, participant observation and ethnography, focus group analysis, observation techniques, and case study analysis."

URBAN DESIGN PRACTICE: Taught by Sinclair Black. "Urban Design creates the vision of synergy, of quality, of economic development, of tax base creation, and of sustainability. The class will involve lectures, videos, a walking tour of San Antonio and several walks in downtown Austin."

URBAN DESIGN

Until 2004, urban design study at UT was included under a MS in Architectural Studies or as a focus in the MArch track. Faculty, including Simon Atkinson and Sinclair Black, taught studios on urban design, infrastructural planning, and urban housing. Today, urban design is available as three degree offerings: MS in Urban Design (MSUD), a post-professional MArch, and a MSUD and MSCRP dual degree. Faculty and students take particular interest in the role of sustainability, landscape, and technology in design problems at the urban scale. The Dallas Urban Laboratory, established in 2006 by Dean Almy, engages in ongoing research and visualization of the city's future urban environment with planners, developers, municipal authorities and community groups.

Above: Hye Kyung Lee, a post-professional urban design student, speaks at the DUL presentation, 2008

Right: Dallas Urban Lab model, 2008

Model, Simon Atkinson, critic, 2000

Chad Gnant, Alexander Kone, Michelle Slattery, Shawn Strange, Ji Zhou, Cedars Reconnect Revitalize, Urban Land Institute Competition: Simon Atkinson, critic, 2008

PERSPECTIVE LOOKING NORTHWEST

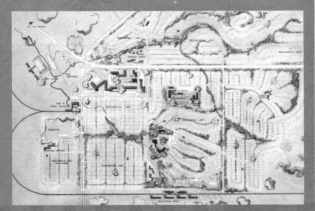

Burnet Plan, 1950

INTERDISCIPLINARY COLLABORATION

Between 1947 and 1950, architecture and planning students created plans and surveys for the city of Burnet, Texas in association with the Bureau of Business Research and the university extension office. Such collaborations continue today in activities like the Urban Land Institute (ULI) Gerald D. Hines Student Urban Design Competition, an annual, graduate-level, interdisciplinary competition. Self-formed teams are composed of students from many fields, including architecture, urban planning, historic preservation, landscape architecture, engineering, development, law, and finance. The teams are asked to provide an urban design and financial feasibility proposal for a large-scale site in the United States. ULI Projects submitted by teams from the school were finalists in 2008 and 2005 and received honorable mentions in 2010, 2007, and 2006.

Popsicle Wars:
Sticky Fingers Snatch a Sweet Metaphor

Terry Kahn, David Bruton, Jr., Centennial Professor in Urban Design; Associate Dean,
Office of the Dean of Graduate Studies; Distinguished Teaching Professor. Faculty member since 1970.

THE SETTING: Hal Box and I team-taught a graduate course on land development in Spring 1997. Though common in the School of Architecture today, such a joint effort between an architect and a planner was an experiment at the time. The theme of the course was what today is called modified New Urbanism, which, by the way, is neither "new" nor "urban."[1] The text was James Kunstler's *Home from Nowhere*, a work positing the general thrust, if not the detail, of the burgeoning New Urbanism.[2] A student asked for a definition of a neighborhood, and I replied, drawing on personal experience from my childhood:

A neighborhood is a place where a kid on a bicycle can get a popsicle within five minutes.

A few days later, the Austin chapter of the Urban Land Institute held one of the early conferences on New Urbanism. Andrés Duany, the featured speaker, was vehement and vitriolic in his critique of urban planning, and Hal Box was on the panel of speakers. Box included the five-minute popsicle in his speech, citing me as the source, but he stated the definition slightly differently:

A neighborhood is a place where a child can walk and get a popsicle within five minutes.

Since then, Box, focused on functionality, and I, focused on economic feasibility, have been happy to let the two definitions speak for themselves. *In Think Like an Architect*, Box has invigoratingly expanded his to a breadth of urban land uses.[3] I continue to defend the original popsicle in class meetings, presentations, and conferences.

The Popsicle as a Description, Not a Prescription

Box and I originally offered our popsicle statements as descriptions of neighborhoods, but over the years others have taken up the definition and sought to apply it as a rule—a prescription for the accomplishment of an agenda. The prime offenders are proponents of New Urbanism, Traditional Neighborhood Development (TND), Smart Growth, and other associated buzzword approaches to urban development. There is even a stock market analyst who has turned it into an index for measuring the health of the financial world. The following examples indicate the burdens placed on the humble popsicle.

1. Randall Bartlett,
   Professor of Economics, Smith College, 2003
   "Finally, there is the 'popsicle test.' An eight-year-old in the neighborhood should be able to walk to a store to buy a popsicle without having to deal with fast moving cars."[4]

Bartlett's paper, titled "Testing the Popsicle Test," is a thorough investigation of the extent to which walk-only customers represent a sufficient volume of business to insure the economic viability of the local retail and other establishments that are the heart of New Urbanism. His conclusion is that walk-only customers cannot support local businesses, a result now recognized by advocates of TND.

2. Davis, California,
   Planning Commission Hearing, 18 May 2005
   "Finally, there is the 'popsicle test.' An eight-year-old in the neighborhood should be able to bike to the store to buy a popsicle without having to battle highway-size streets and freeway-speed traffic."[5]

The statement was from a commissioner in response to a question concerning the extent that the city's regulatory standards would have to be compromised in order to approve a proposed development designed to match New Urbanist principles.

3. Kathleen Falk,
   Dane County, Wisconsin, County Executive, 1998
   "...and finally, the 5-minute popsicle rule—a community is growing successfully when any kid there is within a 5-minute walk to buy a popsicle."[6]

This is a county executive's address at the conclusion of a county planning workshop devoted to land use and environmental policy in a group of growing communities.

4. Lynda Hikichi,
   Regional Planner, Los Angeles County, 2003
   "As described by the Congress for New Urbanism (CNU), if an eight-year-old child in the neighborhood is able to bike to a store and buy a popsicle without having to battle highway-size streets and freeway-speed traffic, the neighborhood is new urbanist."[7]

Hikichi was a student at the University of Wisconsin-Milwaukee and wrote a course paper on transportation and new urbanism which included the popsicle reference.

5. *Omaha World-Herald*, 2006
   "...and he said the New Urbanists like to say the plan should pass the 'Popsicle Test'—that an eight-year-old can walk somewhere for a popsicle without having to cross busy streets."[8]

This is from a newspaper article interview concerning debate over a proposed 160-acre development of previously undeveloped land.

6. Catherine Fitts, Stock Market Analyst, 2003
   "The Popsicle Index is the % of people in a community who believe that a child can leave their home, go to the nearest place to buy a popsicle, and come home safely."[9]

Ms. Fitts uses the popsicle to tie in detailed fashion the health of the community to the health of the stock market.

It is apparent that development interests, both public and private, have adopted varying versions of the popsicle for their own purposes. But note how they have violated one or more parts of the original description, which included:

1) a five-minute limit on access
2) bicycling or walking for transportation
3) a "kid" or "child" for a demographic
4) neighborhood geographical reference.

1) Some statements make no mention of the five-minute or any other time limit and, thus, seriously alter the concept of neighborhood suggested by the original description.

2) There are numerous circumstances that allow safe access on foot or bicycle but require far more time than is normally regarded as viable for non-vehicular local access. Barrett asserts that a walking time of fifteen minutes is the maximum that persons will undertake for local shopping and service access.

3) The words "eight-year-old" specify a narrow demographic. If one wants to depict a "kid" or a "child," an eight-year-old is as good a representation as any. The problem with the narrow depiction is that a neighborhood is comprised of persons across the breadth of ages, including teen-agers and adults, groups that can travel either further or less far than the precisely chosen eight-year–old.

4) Geographic references range from "home" to "community" to "somewhere." These non-neighborhood references miss the point of the popsicle, because they ignore the cohesive and identifiable nature of a neighborhood. That Box's expansion of the popsicle logically extends the neighborhood to larger-scale commercial and residential development perhaps gives the popsicle more power than it is due, but that shouldn't give license to ignore the neighborhood completely.

The Seductive Popsicle

It is amazing that a simple definition of a neighborhood has spawned so much attention with regard to issues of urban development. It is testament to the seductive nature of the popsicle itself—a quiescently frozen confection—that it has been appropriated for such a variety of uses. It is unfortunate that the very popularity of the popsicle has led to so many loose interpretations or flat-out wrong applications. What would have been the response, if any, had the original question for the definition of a neighborhood been answered as follows?

"A neighborhood is a place where a kid on a bicycle can get a box of detergent within five minutes."

---

[1] *Online TDM Encyclopedia – New Urbanism*, August 27, 2007 (http://www.vtpi.org/tdm/tdm24.htm), accessed 2008 from Victoria Transport Institute; Treasure Coast Regional Planning Council, "Sustainable Neighborhood Planning for the Region: The Neighborhood Center and Edge," 2004.

[2] James H. Kuntsler, *Home from Nowhere* (New York: Touchstone, 1996).

[3] Hal Box, *Think Like an Architect* (Austin: University of Texas Press, 2007).

[4] Randall Barrett, "Testing the Popsicle Test: Realities of Retail Shopping in Neo- Traditional Neighbourhood Development," *Urban Studies* 40, no. 8 (July 2003), 1471-1485.

[5] Davis, California, Planning Commission Hearing, May 18, 2005 (www.city.davis.ca.us/covell/pdfs/PC-18-May-question-list-with-answers.pdf), accessed 2008.

[6] Kathleen Falk, "Comments on Dane Growing Strong Workshops," March 11, 1998, (http://www.co.dane.wi.us/exec/landuse/wrapup.htm), accessed 2008.

[7] Lynda Hikichi, New Urbanism and Transportation, Course CE790, University of Wisconsin-Milwaukee, December 2003.

[8] *Omaha World-Herald*, September 10, 2006.

[9] Catherine Austin Fitts, "A Conversation about the Popsicle Index," 2003, (http://www.ratical.com/co-globalize/popsicleIdx.html#p1), accessed 2010.

Teaching Planners to Think Historically about Sustainability

Elizabeth J. Mueller, Assistant Professor. Faculty member since 2000.
Sarah Dooling, Assistant Professor. Faculty member since 2008.

THE PLANNING FIELD has embraced the call to attend to the ecological consequences of metropolitan development patterns. Planners now advocate for more compact development patterns aimed at reducing travel by car while enhancing the function of urban ecosystems. The field's professional organizations have developed policy guidelines and model practices aimed at achieving these goals. In the academy, our students are pushing us to teach them how to practice in this new context. They ask us what the ingredients of a sustainable city are and what elements should be routinely included in plans for cities and sub-districts. They are searching for strategies to foster densification of existing areas of cities. Yet the history of U.S. planning should give us pause. Past urban renewal programs have attempted to remake cities, to draw residents and investment back from the suburbs, and to match an image of modernity we have now discarded. In so doing, some have produced large-scale displacement, especially of minority residents and communities, often reinforcing patterns of segregation that we struggle with to this day. Achieving the goals of sustainability will require us to integrate attention to current problems with visions for the future. We are challenged, as teachers and researchers, to integrate our work across functional areas of planning (such as economic development, housing, and transportation) and across past, present, and future. At the same time, we must attend to the political realities of planning.

Arguably, we face two sorts of challenges in planning for urban sustainability: changing our own thinking about how to plan, and challenging local political forces favoring growth over other goals. Despite our strongly held desire to focus on environmental concerns, planning still takes place in a political context where local governments often are weak and lack resources. As Clarence Stone argues in his classic work on urban politics in Atlanta, neither governmental institutions nor private business interests have the ability to carry out major policy objectives alone; thus, they join together to form governing coalitions in order to assemble the support and resources necessary to accomplish change.[1] Such coalitions bridge the public and private realms, bringing together formal and informal actors and groups in order to build or maintain support for a specific policy agenda. Their stability is based on their ongoing access to valuable resources. Case-study research has emphasized the power of development interests and other business organizations in setting local political agendas. Groups without either organized constituents or valued resources have found it difficult to be included in governing regimes. In a few cases, groups interested in redistributive policies have been able to gain control of decision making for periods, enabling them to follow very different local agendas. Typically, however, continuation of such policies requires ongoing mobilization of supporters across election cycles—and has proven difficult to achieve.

While sustainability ostensibly integrates attention to environmental functionality with the goals of economic prosperity and social equity, it will likely be difficult to prioritize equity concerns if they conflict with strategies narrowly focused on maximizing property values that bring profits to developers and tax revenue to public coffers. Community and Regional Planning Professor Michael Oden argues that only when local environmental advocates join forces with local equity advocates to form durable coalitions will we see a change in priorities.[2] In addition to the political role equity advocates can play in helping build support for new sustainability-focused political agendas, we argue that equity goals must be integrated into plans themselves in order to achieve ecological goals. For example, greater attention to the housing needs of low-income households during periods of rapid growth in Austin might have prevented the parallel and dramatic growth in mobile home settlement in the city's floodplains.

Many planning programs, including ours, are thinking hard about how to reshape curriculum in this new context. Through recent research on planning in Austin, we have identified four specific conceptual challenges that hinder our ability to connect sustainability to existing problems, in particular to patterns of social and environmental vulnerability in central city neighborhoods. These challenges include: reconciling the future orientation of plans with historical processes and context; reconciling the physical and geographic focus of plans with social and historical processes shaping communities that are not observable at that level; understanding how social and environmental conditions have been created or produced; and, finally, understanding the implicit calculus of the public interest embodied by plans.

Future Orientation of Sustainability Plans

The central purpose of sustainability-inspired planning is to reduce the impact of human settlement on various environmental systems and associated ecosystem services. As defined in the United Nations' 2005 Millennium Ecosystems Assessment report, ecosystem services are environmental services from which people benefit.[3] Such services support human health and well-being and include clean air and water, shelter and timber, as well as recreation and spiritual experiences. Public discussion has focused intensely on strategies aimed to reduce human impacts on ecosystems by certain deadlines. The central goal has been lowering the production of greenhouse gases. Planners have focused primarily on the role of transportation, particularly automobiles, and the relationship between land use and travel behavior. Efforts to diagnose causes have been broad brush and aimed at global or regional metrics. The American Planning Association has translated this into a series of policy statements on climate change, sustainability, and smart growth. The emphasis is forward looking and focuses on achieving future goals.

While planning is inherently forward looking, historical analysis is critical to the development of effective plans. It enables us to understand the external context and internal dynamic of problems. Scholars identify several problematic features of practice, including inattention to an issue's own past, a failure to think about key assumptions, and lack of effort to see choices as part of a historical sequence. In the case of sustainability, the key challenges revolve around defining the appropriate past and identifying the ongoing dynamics that have produced current conditions. Since sustainability plans often suggest new roles for agencies and new types of activities, looking historically at implementation and relationships among key elements of the community will be critical to success. This approach would enable a more natural incorporation of existing problems and how they have been produced. Finally, historical analysis makes us more skeptical of "off the shelf" solutions, without prior analysis of context.

Physical and Geographic Scope of Plans

A second issue concerns the scope of sustainability plans. Scope refers both to the physical area and to the functional aspects covered by plans, as well as the timeframe considered. Plans are typically spatially focused on particular neighborhoods, districts, or corridors. The geographic definition of planning areas allows for easy identification of physical conditions and resident groups. However, these administrative planning boundaries should not delimit the processes affecting the area. Nor will all of the community facilities or institutions serving an area be found within its boundaries. Identification of spatial boundaries with existing conditions is especially problematic for understanding social inequities and vulnerabilities.

The Production of Social and Environmental Conditions

To understand how current conditions were created, we must identify and assess the processes related to them. For example, how did a particular area of a city become the site of particular environmental problems or home to particular populations? Without this broader analysis, vulnerabilities become localized problems to be solved, rather than problems produced by ongoing processes, some of which extend beyond administrative boundaries. Problems are observed in a particular place but are not necessarily resolvable at the level of that place. We suspect this results in the displacement of particular features of vulnerability to new sites, rather than improved socio-environmental system functioning. The growing understanding of cities as resilient social and physical systems that change across scales has not yet permeated planning practice.

The Public Interest—Who Benefits and Who Pays

Plans that focus on improving environmental quality are assumed to benefit all. Environment is taken, in essence, to represent the unified public interest. Yet there are other, less clearly unitary forms of public interest embodied in these proposals. Plans that foster more compact urban development, for example, will change the value of property in centrally located areas. Increased property values will have contradictory effects on various "publics." First, city residents will benefit from increased property tax revenues. The benefits will be greatest for those most reliant on public services supported by property taxes, such as schools, city clinics, or local parks. In addition, central city property owners will see the value of their property increase, with the greatest increases going to owners of properties along newly designated transit lines or in gentrifying neighborhoods. As higher values drive up taxes or rents, those least able to afford them—low-income renters and elderly, low-income homeowners—will remain in central neighborhoods at the cost of forgoing other basic needs. Emphasis on central city development will have the effect of making historically low-income and minority neighborhoods—some formed through segregation and further devalued through federal mortgage insurance policy—dramatically more attractive. Absent explicit strategies for protecting existing residents, they are likely to be pushed out by rising housing costs and will not enjoy resulting improvements. Ironically, the same forces pushing out low-income residents and incentivizing demolition of low-rent housing also push up the per-unit cost of new affordable housing in redevelopment projects.

Our role, as planning educators and researchers, is to bring these challenges into our classrooms and into our research and practice. Austin's current efforts to develop a new comprehensive plan, as well as its ongoing efforts to plan for the expansion of transit, offer us a perfect laboratory for our efforts.

---

[1] Clarence Stone, *Regime Politics: Governing Atlanta 1946-1988* (Lawrence: University of Kansas Press, 1989).

[2] Michael Oden, "Equity: the Forgotten 'E' in Sustainability," in *Pragmatic Sustainability: Theoretical and Practical Tools*, Steven A. Moore, ed. (London: Routledge, 2010).

[3] *Millennium Ecosystem Assessment Report: Ecosystems and Human Well-Being: A Synthesis* (Washington, DC: Island Press, 2005).

Service Learning and Critical Pedagogy in the Planning Curriculum

Bjørn Sletto, Assistant Professor. Faculty member since 2007.
Susana Almanza, Director, PODER

PLANNING EDUCATORS face a vexing dilemma: how to teach technical proficiency while also encouraging and furthering students' critical thinking skills? To respond to this challenge, many planning educators turn to service-learning and experiential field courses. Service-learning offers opportunities for planning and design students to work directly with community organizations and address challenging issues of importance to cities and neighborhoods "in the field." In the process, students learn research, planning, and design methods while assisting community-based organizations in their work.[1]

In the spring semester of 2007, I developed such a course in partnership with the community organization People Organized in Defense of Earth and Her Resources (PODER, http://www.poder-texas.org), which works to address environmental justice issues in East Austin. My students were tasked with solving a specific research problem—how to document children's environmental knowledge and perceptions through participatory mapping—while also developing critical, self-reflexive approaches to community engagement. Such an emphasis on critical reflection and flexibility was crucial in this class, since PODER was a well-established authority on East Austin and also had developed successful models for community engagement. PODER has been in existence for nineteen

The Place I do not like

Abandoned House

years and has extensive experience with community-based education and leadership development, where younger leaders learn from their elders, elders learn from young leaders, and the less experienced learn from the more experienced. In order to continue neighborhood traditions and maintain a collective cultural memory, PODER expects leaders to promote communication and mutual respect between elders and youth. The organization also firmly believes that community organizing must come from the grassroots level and that people of color and the poor must participate as equal partners at every level of local, state, federal, national, and international government.

As an educator, this meant striking an appropriate balance between the interests and routines of PODER, the pedagogical standards in the School of Architecture, and technical requirements imposed by the research project. Students had to develop appropriate methods to work with children to best document their knowledge and perceptions of their environment, but they also needed to work effectively and equitably with PODER. This required the students to learn the necessary techniques to solve methodological problems, while also learning how to be open, flexible, and self-reflective in their engagements with PODER and community members. It was an opportunity for students to begin developing into

what Donald Schön called "reflective practitioners."[2] As Schön suggested more than twenty years ago, reflective practitioners are better able to navigate messy planning processes where they must build partnerships through effective communicative strategies, while also contending with different and sometimes conflicting forms of knowledge, perspectives, and interests.

To develop such reflective practitioners through service-learning and field pedagogy, it behooves educators to go beyond focusing students' attention on the "problem" at hand (i.e. the issue to be researched, the plan to be developed, and so on). They might also encourage students to think critically about how knowledge is produced in such experiential field courses, and what role they, as budding professional planners, play within these processes. In such courses, research methods and protocols are subject to intense negotiations between students, faculty members, and community members, and the final representations resulting from such courses—maps, data tables, texts, images, posters, and so on—are similarly contentious. In service-learning courses, students should not merely learn to argue for certain approaches and develop analytical and technical skills. They should also learn to reflect critically on their own identities and positions in the world and in the planning field. This, in turn, allows them to develop

Left: *The Place I Do Not Like*, student neighborhood study, Zavala Elementary School, 2007

Right: Mental map of Zavala Elementary School neighborhood, 2007

the necessary interpersonal skills to facilitate their engagements with community members.

But what are appropriate pedagogical methods for achieving such open and critical reflections about difficult issues of identity, gender, and race, while still imparting the technical skills required in a professional planning curriculum? In my own work, I have found it useful to draw on critical pedagogy, which emphasizes the importance of providing students with new, challenging, and unexpected encounters as part of the learning process—but also the importance of open and supportive reflection activities, which allow students to draw lessons from such encounters.

Critical pedagogy is influenced by the work of the Brazilian educator Paulo Freire, who challenged what he called the "banking concept" of education, where students are merely taught what is considered the necessary and appropriate theoretical framework and technical tools of a given discipline.[3] Instead, critical educators emphasize not only technical skills but also critical thinking and self-reflection. Critical educators draw on a variety of teaching techniques to effect such reflexivity, such as blogging, debriefing sessions, and classroom discussions to inform and make sense of experiences "in the field." They engage consciously with the different stories, experiences, and perspectives students bring to the classroom; they create a supportive space for conversations about sensitive topics such as race and gender, and they openly discuss their own subjectivities as educators.

Perhaps most importantly, instead of attempting to avoid complex or difficult encounters outside the classroom, critical educators use such experiences to encourage students to reflect about what happened, and why. Allowing for the unexpected means giving up control and authority, to the point where teaching and learning become almost indistinguishable processes. Such a democratic classroom experience requires students to take their own knowledge, and also the knowledge of their classmates and community members, more seriously. This, in turn, encourages students to embrace adaptability and flexibility as key attitudes when working with the public and to consider how knowledge is negotiated and developed through interactions between different actors. Ultimately, the principal goal of such critical service-learning is not to teach "skills" per se, but to develop students' ability to think critically about the narratives of people and places that shape their own identities, and, hence, shape their engagements with marginalized and overlooked communities.

Critical pedagogy is particularly appropriate for the sort of participatory environmental justice research we did in my Applied Graphic Information Systems (GIS) class in the spring of 2007. The class project focused on Zavala Elementary School, which is located directly across the street from Pure Casting, Austin's only full-scale industrial foundry. PODER, Zavala teachers and administrators, and residents have long argued that airborne pollutants from Pure Casting present serious health hazards to the children at Zavala. While air quality measurements conducted by the Texas Commission for Environmental Quality suggest that the emissions levels are "moderate," community activists point out that Zavala was built thirty-two years before the foundry and that any chemical emissions at all are unacceptable in a residential neighborhood.

Research in the field of public health also suggests that academic performance can be negatively affected by air pollutants and that children are known to be more adversely affected by environmental pollutants than adults. In addition to being more vulnerable to air pollution than adults, children also spend more time walking and exploring than adults and are therefore more likely to be exposed to hazardous places. From the perspective of PODER, then, the existence of Pure Casting in East Austin is a direct result of segregationist zoning practices in the early twentieth century, which located polluting industries and communities of color

Children's Perception of Safety Near [Zavala Elementary] School by Point and Block: Applied GIS, Bjørn Sletto, critic, 2007

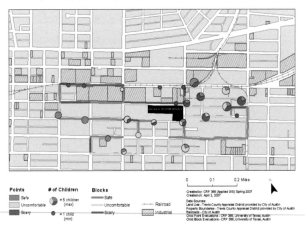

on the East Side, while environmental restrictions were imposed in the western half of the city.

The goal of the class was to document where and how fifth graders at Zavala walk, play, and explore the neighborhood around the school, and also to assess their awareness of any environmental hazards in the area. Students worked closely with PODER and educators at Zavala to develop research methods and strategies appropriate for fifth-grade students, such as storyboarding and simple mapping methods. School of Architecture students and PODER volunteers walked with Zavala students in small groups, carrying street maps and forms that the children could use to map and qualitatively assess locations that they deemed important. Following the field research, one team of UT students developed a systematic approach to transferring the children's spatial and qualitative observations into a GIS, which was made available for download and viewing on a website developed by another class team (http://soa.utexas.edu/eaejp/). An award from the Association of American Geographers and matching funding from the UT Office of the Vice President for Research allowed the students to travel to the association's international conference in San Francisco to present their project and meet with environmental justice and participatory GIS scholars.

During this class, the students and I faced many unexpected challenges that led to lengthy but, ultimately, pedagogically productive discussions. One set of challenges concerned the appropriateness of methods for field work and data analysis, including the appropriate language to use with fifth graders, and we all felt the pressure of the long hours as we tried to meet the expectations of our project partners. But the most profound reflections stemmed from our engagement with PODER and Zavala. Students realized that our own goals and the expectations of community partners were not only different—they were often unsaid, they were embedded in ways of speaking that were unfamiliar to the other, or they were built into assumptions of

Zavala Elementary School students working on neighborhood survey forms, 2007

the "best" and most appropriate ways of conducting research and strategies for publishing research data. Even with extensive pre-planning, we had moments of misunderstanding between students, PODER, Zavala administrators and me. These moments, in turn, provided fodder for critical reflections in the classroom and strengthened students' understanding of their own positionality and how their identities as planning professionals facilitated—and in some ways hindered—their engagement with community organizations.

Such pedagogy is rigorous and time-consuming and requires students and educators to constantly adjust to unexpected and challenging situations both in and out of the classroom. Still, the benefits of such critical approaches to service-learning and experiential field courses extend far beyond environmental justice and the planning field. When teachers and students conceptualize knowledge production as a reciprocal and collaborative endeavor, such an integrated approach to teaching, learning, and doing can have profound, pragmatic value for planning practice. By developing students' understanding of the social contingencies of knowledge production, we facilitate their future engagements with community members.

[1] The authors wish to acknowledge the support of the Association for American Geographers and UT Vice President for Research, Juan Sanchez; fifth-grade teacher Guillermo Barrera for facilitating the field research at Zavala; and Johnny Limon for his introduction to East Austin.

[2] Donald A. Schön, *The Reflective Practicioner: How Professionals Think in Action* (New York: Basic Books, 1983).

[3] Paulo Freire, *Pedagogy of the Oppressed*, trans. Myra Bergman Ramos (New York: Seabury Press, 1970).

The China Planning Workshop

Ming Zhang, Associate Professor. Faculty member since 2004.

WHAT STARTS HERE CHANGES THE WORLD. The banner on the University of Texas' homepage promotes the university and Austin as a place of ideas that attracts people from all over the world, who come to learn, discover, and innovate. For decades, the School of Architecture has offered multi-disciplinary, international, collaborative teaching and learning programs that carry out the energy and aspiration expressed by the banner, reaching out to the rest of the world.

This essay describes the international studios and workshops jointly organized by Community and Regional Planning (CRP) and other disciplines in the school and on the campus. The joint efforts have taken place in Santo Domingo, Dominican Republic; Lima, Peru; Madrid, Spain; and half a dozen Chinese cities. The China program, my focus here, has been carried out annually since 2005.

China's phenomenal economic growth and immense urbanization since 1978 has astonished the world. The China Planning Workshop was initiated to offer opportunities for UT participants to observe with professional eyes China's development dynamics and to explore rural and urban development issues that face rapidly growing Chinese cities and also have global implications. Each year, the faculty collaborates with a

Ming Zhang and UTSOA China Planning Workshop participants at the Great Wall, 2008

Chinese university to select a client city for the planning workshop. The selected client city is either in the stage of revising its comprehensive development plan or facing specific development/redevelopment challenges for which it welcomes fresh ideas from domestic and international scholars, experts, and practitioners. Once the client city is identified, a team is then assembled consisting of faculty and students from the School of Architecture and the collaborating Chinese university, as well as experts in the locally needed fields.

The workshops/studios are joint efforts with multiple dimensions. First of all, it is a joint educational endeavor between UTSOA and the Chinese universities. Faculty and students from both sides of the Pacific Ocean share course syllabi and work on the same set of tasks for the workshop projects. During the workshop, the student teams mixed UT and Chinese participants, and intermediate and final reviews are held jointly. For the Beijing Studio, fifteen students and three faculty members from UTSOA visited the studio site in Beijing and toured other cities in China in the summer of 2008. In October, 2008, faculty and students from Tsinghua

University traveled to Austin for a mid-term review. On December 11, 2008, the Tsinghua team participated in the UTSOA final review virtually: their design scheme was transmitted through the Internet and presented with recorded audio. In early January of 2009, before the winter semester ended in China, three representatives from Austin participated in the Tsinghua final review. Participants from both universities found the joint studio a very positive and rewarding experience for mutual learning and for curriculum enhancement.

Another dimension of the workshops/studios is interdisciplinarity. They involve students and faculty from multiple disciplines, including planning, architecture, landscape architecture, civil engineering, public policy, and geography. By working in teams, the students learn from their peers of different backgrounds and incorporate diverse disciplinary approaches toward problem solving. For instance, when exploring development strategies for the moat area of the ancient Suizhou City, CRP students Martin Thomen and Jeong-il Park and their Chinese teammates studied water quality, waste treatment, and ecosystem planning, whereas architecture students

China Planning Workshop

Year	Client City	Collaborating University	Main Topic
2010	*Wuhan, Hubei Province and Guangzhou, Guangdong Province*	*Wuhan University, Huazhong University of Science & Technology, and South China University of Technology*	*High-Speed Rail and Urban/Regional Development*
2009	*Handan, Hebei Province and Guangzhou, Guangdong Province*	*Huazhong University of Science & Technology, and South China University of Technology*	*Fengfeng District Plan and Brownfield Redevelopment*
2008	*Beijing*	*Tsinghua University*	*Neighborhood Redevelopment and Network of Pocket Parks*
2007	*Suizhou, Hubei Province*	*Huazhong University of Science & Technology*	*Suizhou City Comprehensive Plan Revision and Historical District Preservation*
2006	*Guangshui, Hubei Province*	*Huazhong University of Science & Technology*	*Guangshui City Comprehensive Plan Revision and Waterfront Redevelopment*
2005	*Ji'an, Jiangxi Province*	*Huazhong University of Science & Technology*	*Ji'an City Comprehensive Plan Revision*

Margaret Saunders and Patricia Boucher focused on design schemes for different moat segments and nodes. International best practice examples such as the Riverwalk in San Antonio, Texas, and the waterfront development in Chattanooga, Tennessee, were introduced to illustrate the planning and design ideas. During the Beijing studio, design students first worked together with planning students in projecting demographic, economic, and housing demand trends of the study area. In the later stage of the studio, planning students practiced design techniques to translate planning ideas into physical and spatial objects.

Furthermore, the workshop is a joint effort between academia and local officials and professionals on pressing issues facing local community development. Aside from receiving logistical support (room, board, and local transportation) from the client city, the participants have the opportunity to work shoulder-to-shoulder with local professionals in seeking desirable solutions to the problems facing the city. The international collaboration contributes to producing high-quality urban plans and design solutions. The joint teams have delivered products that are above and beyond the standard list of maps and documents specified by the planning guideline issued by China's Ministry of Construction. Furthermore, for each workshop, the teams study a set of topics of interest for planning in both the United States and China. Examples of the topics are Plan Quality and Plan Evaluation, Brownfield Redevelopment, and High-Speed Rail and Urban/Regional Spatial Development Strategies.

Through learning by doing, the students have gained insights to China's development issues far beyond textbook descriptions, witnessing in person urban development in this era of rapid economic growth. The workshop and related travel has been an eye-opening

Tsinghua University China Planning Workshop team at the Austin City Hall, 2008

experience to the participants who were in China for the first time. They learn further about Chinese history and culture from visiting a variety of places, ranging from the Forbidden City in Beijing to the thousand-year-old villages in Ji'an of Jiangxi Province. Alex Kone, a CRP student, articulated the reaction of many of his fellow students in his Study Tour Report:

There has always been a lack of superlatives to explain the magnitude of China's economic growth since 1978. The centuries and millennia that have passed have yet to grasp the sheer extent of the size of the country and the scale to which it undertakes the construction of its great projects, including its cities...

In the past six years, more than sixty UT students, one hundred Chinese students, and thirty local Chinese planners have participated in the China Program. The SOA faculty organizing the workshops/studios includes professors Kent Butler, Robert Paterson, Fritz Steiner, Wilfried Wang, and Ming Zhang. Financial support to the workshop comes from the client city and the Hampton K. and Margaret Frye Snell Endowed Chair in Transportation.

The Latin American Connection

The School of Architecture has had a prominent role in UT's enduring relationship with Mexico and other Latin American countries. The path runs two ways, with faculty and students venturing south and new students and visiting critics making the trip north to Goldsmith Hall.

In 1934, a Peruvian architecture student named Fernando Belaúnde Terry (BArch '35) transferred to UT from the University of Miami to complete his degree under the mentorship of Walter Rolfe. Upon his return to Peru he practiced and taught architecture, founded a professional journal (*El Arquitecto Peruano*), and became an authority on government and public housing before embarking on a political career in which he served two terms as the nation's president (1963-68, 1980-85). During his presidency in 1965, Belaúnde bestowed Rolfe with Peru's highest honor, the Order of the Sun, for "outstanding contribution to the furtherance of architectural education and practice in Peru."

Hugh McMath, who followed Rolfe as chairman in 1946, also had a deep interest in Latin American culture and architecture. Over his forty-four-year teaching career at UT, he developed courses in pre-Columbian and Spanish colonial architecture in Mexico and led workshops in conjunction with Mexican universities. Among these was a summer program at the Instituto Tecnológico de Monterrey that was attended by students from around the U.S.

Hal Box, whose interest in Latin America began during his student days at UT, pursued the subject as Dean. In 1988, he and Logan Wagner began a twelve-year project with Earthwatch to document open-air churches and other civic spaces in Mexico. He also encouraged Sinclair Black to establish the school's Studio Mexico program, which, since 1998, has been led by Juan Miró. The studio includes students from a variety of the school's disciplines, including architecture, landscape architecture, and historic preservation. They travel to Mexico for a month visiting historic and contemporary architecture, meeting with students from Mexican schools of architecture, and attending lectures by prominent Mexican architects. Upon their return to Austin, they complete a project that often is on a topic being examined by their Mexican counterparts. Final reviews sometimes are held jointly.

President Fernando Belaúnde Terry (BArch '35) and Lady Bird Johnson share a laugh after Belaúnde's speech on campus, 1985

Rolfe receives the Order of the Sun from UN delegate, Dr. Javiar Correa-Elias, 1965

Faculty and students from a design workshop at the Instituto Tecnológico de Monterrery, 1952. Hugh McMath is fourth from the left in the back row.

Other initiatives include an inter-session design/ build project in 2005, in which Sergio Palleroni and Steven Moore worked with thirty-nine students building houses exemplifying principles of cultural, economic, and environmental sustainability for a community of Yaqui Indians in Sonora, Mexico. In 2006 this program was featured in the "Green for All" episode of the PBS series *Design e2*. Since 2008, Bjørn Sletto, Kent Butler, and Ming Zhang have been involved with a service-learning program in Santo Domingo, Dominican Republic. And in 2009 and 2010, the Center for American Architecture and Design hosted the Latitudes Symposium bringing to campus a diverse range of architects from North, Central, and South America to debate the question of whether there is—already, still emerging, or never to be —a distinctly "American" modern architecture.

Juan Miró with students from UT and from the Universidad de Veracruzana at the house of Mexican architect Ricardo Fernandez, Veracruz, Mexico, 2004

100 Years of (non-) Solitude:
The School of Architecture and Latin America

Fernando Lara, Assistant Professor. Faculty member since 2009.

TO TALK ABOUT THE long-standing relationship between the School of Architecture and Latin America I found no better framework than García Márquez's literary masterpiece, *One Hundred Years of Solitude* (1967). His narrative, if you remember, is one in which the passage of time is made extremely flexible, sometimes stalled, sometimes hectic. Characters of vast physical strengths or deep solitude alternate in a city, Macondo, that is at first completely removed from the outside world, as if the nation was built as a constellation floating in the sky. Despite the different paces, there is an overall sense of inevitability.

It is with the idea of inevitability that I want to start this conversation. With Texas being part of a certain geographic continuum around the Gulf of Mexico that dates literally to Jurassic times, it is no wonder that the connections with Latin America run deep. In that kind of timescale, the three centuries of Spanish occupation are a drop in the bucket, but one that forged the cultural ties between Texas and its neighbors to the south. In keeping with this cultural tradition the University of Texas is proud to house the best library collection of Latin American titles (Nettie Lee Benson Latin American Collection) and the most respected institute of Latin American Studies (Teresa Lozano Long Institute of Latin American Studies—LLILAS) in the country.

Despite so much in common there is, nevertheless, a strong component of isolation, that other backbone of

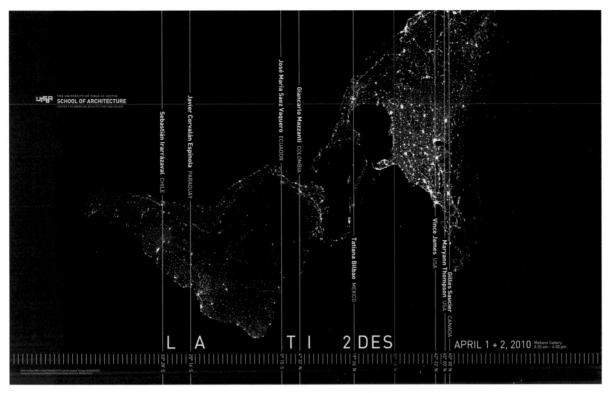

Latitudes 2010 symposium poster, Center for American Architecture and Design, designed by Cameron Kraus

García Márquez's novel. Devastating centrifugal forces of modernity run through Macondo as it did throughout Latin America, transforming the idyllic place forever. In architecture that translates to a fascination with colonial architecture, mostly seen through the lens of idyllic old times. Another obsession is a dual-faced attraction to modernism and its contradictions, reflecting and refracting those twentieth-century transformations. The School of Architecture has followed those traditions, sometimes with a hectic pace and other times with more spaced exchanges. As a consequence, the isolation is broken and a network of relationships inevitably carries information back and forth. A constellation is mapped.

According to emeritus professor and former dean Hal Box (BArch '50), interest in Latin America was present at the school from its early years but became strongly visible in the 1940s. At that time, says Hal, architects were fascinated with the fact that Mexico was way ahead in modernism, and Brazil was being praised for its modern ingenuity. *Brazil Builds*, the catalogue of the Museum of Modern Art's 1943 exhibition that first introduced Brazilian modernism to the world, was the first book that Hal remembers buying as a student

here.[1] Such interest grew in the 1950s as regional modernism gained momentum. O'Neil Ford, for instance, collaborated with Félix Candela and was very interested in Mexican architecture.

At the same time that Latin American architecture was making an impact at the school, our graduates were having a significant role in different parts of Latin America. A number of students from Mexico and Central American states attended the school, and the large majority of them returned to practice architecture in their homelands. Among them was the only UT alumnus to reach a national executive office. Fernando Belaúnde Terry was born in Lima in 1912. After graduating in 1936 he returned to Peru, founded a magazine, became an advocate for public housing, and was elected to congress in 1945. In 1963, he was elected president of Peru and is credited with being the strongest promoter of modernism in his country.

Interestingly, the era of the 1960s and 1970s was a time in which the architecture of Latin America was no longer making headlines. The turmoil of the cold war rippled strongly over Latin America and political instability became the norm. Architecture (here and elsewhere) had other interests and the exchange slowed considerably. The 1980s, however, would see a tidal change that brought Latin American issues strongly back into the school. In 1981, Patricia Wilson began the graduate dual-degree program between Community and Regional Planning and the Institute for Latin American Studies. With its success, the Sociedad Interamericana de Planificación was based in the school in the1990s under the leadership of Wilson. Now directed by Bjørn Sletto, the dual-degree program has to date graduated more than one hundred planners with a concentration on Latin American cities.

Also in the 1980s, Hal Box obtained support from EarthWatch to run a large program documenting public spaces in Mexico. For twelve summers, two teams of fifteen people worked in Mexican cities, surveying and drawing a total of ninety plazas. The initiative developed into a regular studio with a focus on Mexico, first directed by Sinclair Black and Logan Wagner and now led by Juan Miró. The integration of studio, history, and visual communication in a focused traveling course provides an intensity and richness of experience unmatched by any of its components in isolation.

With the turn of the millennium, Latin American issues have found even more space at the school. Since 2002, Wilfried Wang and Barbara Hoidn have added several studios in South America to the pool of courses. A series of O'Neil Ford publications (the duograph series) have focused on Chile (2008) and Brazil (2009).[2] In addition, the Latitudes conferences organized by the Center for American Architecture & Design have twice (in 2009 and 2010) brought to the school some of the best architects from all over the Americas, North and South, elevating the conversation about what it means to do architecture in the New World. A recent lecture series co-sponsored with LLILAS marking the fiftieth anniversary of Brasília was the latest addition to the remarkable engagement between the school and our southern neighbors.

As for the future of Latin American architecture at the School of Architecture, I can only go back to García Márquez to explain that we are inevitably and eternally connected to Latin America by geography, by history, and by design culture. If the theme of his book is isolation and solitude, a powerful historical thread runs through it, weaving a constellation. We have a similar constellation here, the assemblage of the many fantastic initiatives of our history. It is our guiding star, we follow its lead.

[1] Philip Lippincott Goodwin, *Brazil Builds: Architecture New and Old, 1652-1942* (New York: Museum of Modern Art, 1943).

[2] Kevin Alter and Wilfried Wang, eds., *O'Neil Ford Duograph 1: Chile: House at Punta Pite, 2003-2006, Smiljan Radic; Crypt in the Cathedral of Santiago de Chile, 1999-2006, Rodrigo Pérez de Arce* (Austin: University of Texas at Austin Center for American Architecture & Design and Tübingen: Ernst Wasmuth Verlag, 2008). Barbara Hoidn and Kevin Alter, eds., *O'Neil Ford Duograph 2: Brazil: House in Rio Bonito, 2002-2005, Carla Juaçaba; House in Santa Teresa, 2005-2008, Angelo Bucci* (Austin: University of Texas at Austin Center for American Architecture & Design and Tübingen: Ernst Wasmuth Verlag, 2009).

Study Abroad

study in italy

Postcard collage of
student work, Study
in Italy Program,
2007

Long-standing study abroad programs led by School of Architecture faculty include Studio Mexico, established by Sinclair Black with Logan Wagner and now led by Juan Miró; the European Study Abroad Program, created by Larry Doll, who can recommend a café in every city on the continent with exemplary modern architecture; the Oxford Study Abroad Program led by Simon Atkinson; and the Italy Program based in Castiglion Fiorentino, Tuscany, directed by Smilja Milovanovic-Bertram, which attracts 30 to 40 percent of each fourth-year class. For many years before her retirement in 2007, Gerlinde Leiding introduced generations of students to Japan. In addition to these regularly offered, semester-long programs, the school has a tradition of occasional courses, such as Ming Zhang's China Planning Workshop, and brief trips for first-hand visits to sites of studio design problems. Undergraduate and graduate students seeking full immersion in another culture often take advantage of the Professional Residency Program, which places students in offices around the world.

History of the Sustainable Design Program, 1973-2010

Michael Garrison, Professor, Cass Gilbert Teaching Fellow in Architecture. Faculty member since 1975.

ECOLOGICAL DESIGN was not new to the School of Architecture in the 1970s. For decades, the school had been incorporating the principles of bioclimatic design, design for solar control (Victor Olgyay, *Design With Climate*, 1963), and the impact of environmental engineering on the design of buildings (Reyner Banham, *Architecture of the Well-Tempered Environment*, 1969) in its approach to architectural regionalism. In fact, the need for shelter and the effects of climate on human environments have been concerns in the architectural curriculum since the beginning of the school. Topics in sustainable design have continued to evolve at the school in response to the ideals of the faculty and students and their perceptions of changing global environmental conditions and political events. In 1965, the school, then led by Philip Creer, organized the Texas Conference on Our Environmental Crisis with the support of the university and Texas Governor John Connelly. Among the participants were Lady Bird Johnson, Senator Gaylord Nelson (Wisconsin), J. B. Jackson, and Philip Johnson.[1]

The 1970s

At the beginning of the 1970s, after millions of Americans witnessed the earth-rise from the view of our astronauts orbiting the moon, there was a renewed sense of environmental conservation sweeping the nation's campuses. In spring 1970, Senator Nelson created the

Pliny Fisk working on a windmill installation at the Architecture Annex, 1973

first Earth Week when twenty million Americans across the nation demonstrated in support of environmental awareness. This movement led to the creation of the United States Environmental Protection Agency (EPA) and the passage of the Clean Air, Clean Water, and Endangered Species Acts.

In 1973, the so-called "oil crisis" started when the members of Organization of Arab Petroleum Exporting Countries proclaimed an oil embargo, and the market price for oil immediately quadrupled. In the United States there was rationing of gasoline, with motorists facing long lines at the gas pumps. The crisis led to greater interest in energy conservation and renewable energy and spurred research in solar and wind power.

In the atmosphere of that time, Dean Charles Burnette brought Pliny Fisk to the school in 1973 to build a program in energy and architecture. Fisk advocated a low-cost building systems approach to architectural materials and methods developed under the tutelage of ecologist and author Ian McHarg (*Design With Nature*,

1969) at the University of Pennsylvania. Fisk's design studios focused on design-build projects, where students worked with adobe walls, caliche blocks, straw-bale structures, rainwater cisterns, wind generators, and low-cost solar collectors. The studio work was housed in the architecture annex, a decommissioned church on the northern edge of campus.

I joined the faculty in 1975 and began teaching passive solar design and technology integration studios in the annex along with Pliny and Daria Bolton Fisk, who formed the Center for Maximum Potential Building Systems (CMPBS) that same year to showcase their work. Over the next two years, I received funding from the U.S. Department of Energy (DOE) and the State of Texas to design-build a series of solar greenhouse structures at the university's Balcones Research Center (now the Pickle Research Campus) in north Austin. These structures proved the feasibility of passive solar systems, thermal storage, and solar-induced ventilation and led to a series of passive-solar demonstration houses funded by the state and the U.S.

A test structure for the Lab for Maximum Potential Building Systems at the Balcones Research Center, 1980.

started the graduate Architecture and Energy program, appointing Arumí-Noe as the program's first director.

In the 1970s, the study of ecological design marked a period of great experimentation at the school, punctuated by a sense that the work was on the cutting edge of the emerging sustainable architecture and planning movement. Studio projects fostering a more symbiotic relationship between architecture and the natural environment that emphasized regional contexts and resource use relative to materials, energy, water, waste, and food influenced a generation of UTSOA graduates.

The 1980s

The second oil crisis in the United States occurred at the end of the decade in 1979 in the wake of the Iranian Revolution. In response to this new crisis, the United States reduced energy demand, and oil prices began a six-year decline that culminated with a 46 percent price drop in 1986, ending a period of economic stagnation and ushering in the beginning of a period of economic expansion. During this time, Dean Box emphasized the professional development of the school, remodeling and enlarging its facilities, and adding endowments and scholarships. He also brought in Charles W. Moore as the O'Neil Ford Centennial Chair. In the design studios, international modernism was being questioned, and the ideas of postmodern architecture portended a shift from the modernist ethos of form-follows-function minimalism to investigations of postmodernist styles and situated regionalism, or what Harwell Hamilton Harris called the "regionalism of liberation."

Department of Housing and Urban Development. Fisk left the university in 1977 to develop the CMPBS as an independent research center, and the design-build studios were taken over for a few years by David Smith, who brought an expertise in adobe and earth-covered building design and construction.

Meanwhile, in Goldsmith Hall, physicist Francisco Arumí-Noe, who joined the faculty in 1974, was teaching architecture courses in thermal design, energy and thermal inertia, and solar geometry, and pioneered the Dynamic Energy Response of Buildings (DEROB) computer simulation program, one of the first national standards for the simulation of building energy performance approved by the DOE. Arumí established the UTSOA Numerical Simulation Laboratory during the mid-1970s and, together with Associate Dean Richard Dodge, co-taught studios that simulated the energy performance of energy-conscious designs. Hal Box became dean in 1976 and provided the leadership that

Adding commercial design expertise to the energy and architecture program, Buford Duke, Jr., joined the faculty in 1981, having recently won the competition for the Sacramento State Office Building (1978), as principal designer with the Benham group. The building was considered at the time one of the pioneering energy-efficient solar office buildings in America. Duke's Green Team studios worked on design projects integrating both passive and active solar systems at different scales from urban master planning to small residential designs. His Gentle Architecture studios also worked on a host of energy-efficient design projects for disadvantaged people including projects for the Peace Corps, Kenya, East Austin, and colonia housing.

Arumí-Noe led the graduate program throughout the 1980s, changing the name of the program to Design

The Architecture Annex on Dean Keeton St. in use from 1972 to 1980.

Francisco Arumí's DEROB software allowed him to evaluate the energy performance of buildings prior to construction, 1980

With Climate to reflect an emphasis on technology integration, passive solar, and regional bioclimatic design in keeping with the school's participation in National Passive Solar Conferences. He received funding to expand DEROB by integrating 3-D solid graphics modeling and energy analysis and to develop enhanced MUSES computer software codes. Additional funded research in the graduate program from the DOE and the Texas Energy and Natural Resources Advisory Council supported my graduate research team to develop regional passive solar guidelines for housing designs that were widely distributed throughout Texas by the state's Public Utility Commission. This research work was integrated into the design studios, and during the decade UTSOA students won numerous state and national awards for their integrated energy-conscious design projects.

In 1989, the Austin City Council appointed me to chair the Resource Management Commission (RMC). I and the RMC, along with Roger Duncan, Lawrence Doxsey, Gail Vittori, Pliny Fisk and others, helped the Resource Management Department (RMD, the conservation division of Austin Energy, the municipally-owned utility) evolve its Energy Star Program into Austin Energy Green Building, the country's first comprehensive green building program. Austin Energy Green Building influenced the creation of the U.S. Green Building Council Leadership in Energy and Environmental Design (LEED) certification in 1998.

The 1990s

In 1990, following Iraq's invasion of Kuwait, the American economy plunged into a recession. The recovery that began in March 1991 inaugurated a sustained period of economic expansion that enabled an unparalleled surge in architectural creativity. Completely new design possibilities were opened up by technological innovations such as computer-aided design and high-tech utilitarianism celebrating innovations in building systems technology.

In 1992, Larry Speck became dean, William McDonough published the Hannover Principles, and the First United Nations Conference on Environment and Development (Earth Summit) was held in Rio de Janeiro ushering in a new paradigm of sustainable design. Sustainable design was defined by the conference as "design that meets the needs of the present generation without compromising the ability of future generations to meet their needs."

To address the challenge of sustainable design, I led a team of graduate students funded by the U.S. Department of the Interior, the National Park Service, and the Park Foundation on a series of sustainable design-build projects in Big Bend National Park in 1994. The design teams developed permanent sustainable housing appropriate to the hot-arid Chihuahuan desert to replace temporary trailers that were being used to house park rangers. The design features included energy and water conservation systems, ramada shading porches, passive solar heating, high thermal mass construction, cooling towers with solar induced ventilation, solar hot water heating, and building-integrated photovoltaic (BIPV) systems. These construction projects were followed in 1996 and 1997 by sustainable design work in collaboration with Buford Duke for colonia housing in South Texas sponsored by the Alamo Area Council of Governments and the Texas Department of Housing and Community Affairs.

2000 The New Millennium

At the beginning of the new millennium, issues of global environmental concern were becoming more important to the American public. Factors such as global warming, air and water pollution, population growth, and loss of habitat biodiversity contributed to a call for sustainable design to become more ubiquitous.

With the deaths of Buford Duke in 2000 and Francisco Arumí-Noe in 2005, the leadership of the program passed on to a new generation. Steven Moore, who had joined the faculty in 1997, was appointed director of the Design with Climate program in 1999. In 2002, he revised the program and changed the name to Sustainable

Design to reflect the program's interconnectedness of environment, economy, and social equity. Three years later, he established the trans-disciplinary Portfolio Program in Sustainability with support from the Henry Luce Foundation. Through his courses and scholarship he has enriched the theoretical dimension of the program by situating sustainable design within broad discourses in philosophy, science and technology studies, and cultural geography. Fritz Steiner, a designer and planner with an extensive background in ecological planning and growth management, became dean in 2001. Like Pliny Fisk, he had been a student of Ian McHarg. Under his leadership, the Sustainable Design program has been strengthened with additional faculty, increased research funding, and new program areas including landscape architecture. New faculty associated with the Sustainable Design program include Ulrich Dangel (2005), Dason Whitsett (2006, BArch '95, MSSD '05), and Matt Fajkus (2010).

In 2001, Steven Moore and Robert Paterson co-founded the Center for Sustainable Development (CSD) to develop creative, balanced, achievable solutions to the physical and social challenges facing the planning, construction, and preservation of buildings, neighborhoods, and regions and to mark a shift in university funding from state support to externally funded research. In 2000, Paterson released the first Central Texas Sustainability Indicators Project (CTSIP), which is now an ongoing part of the CSD. The CTSIP is intended to increase regional awareness and commitment to sustainability by tracking the progress of quality-of-life indicators. Following Moore and Paterson, the CSD has been led by Elizabeth Mueller, who secured funding from the Meadows Foundation to incorporate principles of

2007 Solar Decathlon House on the National Mall

sustainable design into the core UTSOA curriculum, and Werner Lang, who with Assistant Director Barbara Brown Wilson (Interim Director in 2010), launched important initiatives including the Thermal Lab and the Living Lab.

Another significant institutional development has been the addition of the Lady Bird Johnson Wildflower Center, which joined UT in 2007 as part of the School of Architecture and the College of Natural Sciences. Alongside its native plants research, the Wildflower Center is a leader in restoration ecology and green roof design. With the CSD, the American Society of Landscape Architects, the USGBC, EPA and others, the Wildflower Center led the development of the Sustainable Site Initiatives, which are the outdoor equivalent of LEED.

Design-build has remained an important component of the Sustainable Design program. The school entered teams in three Solar Decathlon competitions sponsored by the DOE and National Renewable Energy Laboratory. The 2002 team was led by me and Pliny Fisk, back as a visiting professor; Samantha Randall, Elizabeth Alford, and I headed the 2005 team; and Randall, Russell Krepart (MArch '02), and I directed the 2007 team. Each produced a stand-alone solar house erected on the National Mall in Washington, D.C., that demonstrated state-of-the-art, sustainable-designed, photovoltaic-powered modular housing. The 2007 house now sits on top of Mt. Locke at the university's McDonald Observatory supporting observatory staff in their scientific missions. Alford and I followed up this work with funded research to develop solar powered modular housing prototypes to replace FEMA disaster relief trailers along the Gulf Coast.

The affordable Alley Flat Initiative is another design-build project begun in 2005 under the direction of Moore, Visiting Professor Sergio Palleroni, and Michael Gatto (MArch '01). As of spring 2010, thirteen Alley Flats are at various stages of testing, occupancy, design, and permitting. Funding from the National Science Foundation has supported research by Moore and many graduate students related to the relationship of social equity and technological codes in the context of Alley Flat development in Austin.

In 2007, Moore led a graduate team that won the City of Austin, National Research Idea Competition for ideas for integrating utility infrastructure. The team donated the $250,000 prize to the graduate Sustainable Design program as an Excellence Award to support future interdisciplinary graduate student research.

2010 and Beyond

At the end of the first decade of the new millennium, the Sustainable Design program strives to remain at the cutting edge of teaching and research in sustainable design, while preparing the future leaders of our profession. It is the oldest and one of the largest of any graduate sustainable design programs in the nation and was recently ranked in the top three graduate sustainable design programs in the United States by *Design Intelligence* of the Design Futures Council. At a time when developing clean and renewable energy strategies and addressing ever-increasing energy consumption rates are so crucial to our economic and ecological future, the School of Architecture's Sustainable Design program continues to lead the exploration of ecological and socially and economically responsible building alternatives to truly create a sustainable world.

[1] School of Architecture, *Texas Conference on Our Environmental Crisis*, proceedings, November 1965 (Austin: School of Architecture, University of Texas, 1966).

Experimental Research
at the School of Architecture

Werner Lang, Associate Professor. Faculty member 2008-2010. Director, Lang Hugger Rampp GmbH Architects, Munich.

FORM, SIZE, VOLUME, proportion, scale, color, texture, modulation of light, and creation of space are just a few of the parameters indicating that the creation of architecture is about the definition of our built environment in a physical way. This physical aspect of architecture has traditionally been the primary focus of research in architecture schools, while research related to the thermal performance of buildings was conducted by architectural and structural engineers and rarely connected to the field of architectural exploration.

With the re-discovery of sustainability as one of the core aspects of architecture during the past decade, architects, designers, and planners have begun to see a new venue for research in these fields. These practitioners understand that the urgent need for more sustainable buildings offers a tremendous opportunity to position architecture as a way to create shelter, to define space, and to modulate the climatic conditions so that the physical performance of a building becomes a driving force for design. "Sustainable building" can be understood as the careful balancing of the local conditions with the physical and emotional needs of the user. This offers the chance to create beauty that serves as well as it pleases.

The School of Architecture is known for its enduring work in the fields of sustainable design and development, architecture, urban and landscape design, community and regional planning, and other related programs.

School of Architecture Thermal Lab, 2010

The scope of the work varies in size and focus from the interdisciplinary Master of Science in Sustainable Design program, to the scholarly activities of faculty members, to the applied research programs like the Solar Decathlon, offered to engage students. Based on this rich background and the urgent need to facilitate experimental research related to the maximization of building performance, the school's Thermal Lab was established in 2009 for testing the thermal performance of innovative components, systems, and buildings in hot climates, such as that of Central Texas, and pairing the numeric analysis of energy performance with the qualitative analysis of the structural and aesthetic characteristics of these architectural elements.

The Thermal Lab simulates a full-scale single room with a south-facing facade, allowing for thermal experiments as well as for research in the field of the energy consumption related to comfort, light-control, ventilation, and the direct and indirect use of solar energy. A facility that can measure the effects of facade-material innovations and shading treatments informs the field of experimental research in sustainability in two ways. First, with regard to comfort, energy consumption, and aesthetics, the building envelope is by far the most important subsystem of the building, and its performance dramatically influences the load on building services. Second, predicting a structure's thermal behavior is inherently dependent on using real-scale facilities, as the relation between the building volume and its surface area are decisive aspects with regard to thermal gains and losses that influence the comfort, as well as the related energy demand for the creation of this comfort.

School of
Architecture
Thermal Lab, 2010

Thermal Lab not only allows for exploration under real environmental conditions, but also exposes the lab to the campus community. The value of this experimental facility will be amplified by its dynamic and integrated use by architects, planners, designers, and engineers.

Proper use of this laboratory calls for a multidisciplinary and integrated approach to problem solving by an interdisciplinary team of scientists and students from the fields of architecture, engineering, natural sciences, and other areas. The outdoor placement of the

The proximity to the school's existing facilities, such as the Design Workshops, the Materials Lab, the Computer Lab, the Digital Fabrication Lab, and the Conservation Lab allows for the deployment of immediate and effective design studies that demonstrate the scope and tremendous potential of research in the field of sustainable architecture with regard to comfort, to reduction of the need for fossil fuels, and to the extension of the current limits of architectural design. We hope this experimental research will help to foster and extend the reputation of UT as one of the leading institutions nationwide for sustainable research and design and will attract, inspire, and energize our students to engage with this field and change the future of building.

Historic Preservation
in the School of Architecture

Michael Holleran, Associate Professor. Faculty member since 2006.
Frances Gale, Senior Lecturer; Director, Architectural Conservation Laboratory. Faculty member since 2008.

HISTORIC PRESERVATION has been a part of the School of Architecture nearly from its inception. In 1913, three years after the school's founding, Samuel Gideon came to Austin as the third member of the Architecture faculty, and from then until his death in 1945 he and his students researched the early buildings of Texas. He helped save Austin's French Legation and O. Henry House, two of the earliest preservation efforts in the city, and "discovered Fredericksburg," in the words of Eugene George (BArch '49), who was one of his students. Gideon served on the national AIA Committee on Historic Preservation.

A new era began in the 1950s when Gene George and D. Blake Alexander (BArch '50) joined the faculty. Alexander started teaching here in 1955 and sent his students to measure and draw the historic structures of Texas. These drawings formed the nucleus of what became the Alexander Architectural Archive. George joined the faculty in 1957 and four years later revived the Historic American Buildings Survey (HABS) in Texas, after a twenty-year hiatus. He left Austin in 1962 to head the architecture department at the University of Kansas and later served as Resident Architect for Colonial Williamsburg. He returned to UT in 1975 and taught here in varying capacities until 1997. Blake's and Gene's students are now the leaders of preservation architecture throughout Texas and across the United States.

One of their students was Wayne Bell, FAIA (BArch '60). After some time in private practice, Bell came to work at the university as an architect, initiating efforts to preserve the campus by doing the first restoration plan for the Littlefield Home. When longtime UT benefactor Ima Hogg purchased the 1834 Stagecoach Inn and other historic properties at Winedale in Fayette County and began conversations about donating them to the university, Wayne became the preservation architect for the project. Once the donation was accomplished, he served as the first director of the Winedale Historical Center. The center began hosting Winedale Workshops, scholarly symposia on Texas's historical architecture and its preservation.

Preservation in the 1960s took on a sense of urgency and insurgency that made it attractive to young architects.

Wayne Bell working with students, 1980

Preservationists reacted to the neglect of old cities and towns or their active destruction through urban renewal and highway construction. Architects could devise the solutions to keep old structures sound and useful, and they could appreciate the aesthetic of temporal collage as one alternative to a modernism that was becoming The Establishment. The national preservation movement flowered in 1966, first with the publication of *With Heritage So Rich*, a manifesto with a foreword by Lady Bird Johnson.[1] Later that year, Congress passed the National Historic Preservation Act, establishing the National Register of Historic Places. Wayne Bell moved over to what is now the Texas Historical Commission to set up the National Register program for the State of Texas. Preservation, he recalls, "was brand new, and everyone was jumping on the bandwagon."

The Graduate School began listing Blake Alexander as a professor of Architectural History and Preservation in 1968, the first time preservation appears as a subject in a UT course catalog. The same year, Roy Graham, who had been a campus architect at the University of Virginia, joined the faculty. The following year, at Blake's suggestion, he began offering an advanced studio in Historic Continuity, UT's first preservation studio. "Instead of the traditional, museum-style resurrection," according to an *Alcalde* feature, "historic continuity concentrates on being responsive to the present."[2] Roy's students prepared plans for Austin's Symphony Square, San Antonio's Old Ursuline Academy, and for Guerrero Viejo, Mexico.

Wayne Bell returned to UT in the 1971-1972 academic year to teach Architectural Restoration, the university's first preservation course outside the studio. Bell's courses were offered at first through American Civilization in the College of Liberal Arts, cross-listed with Architecture, and he held a joint appointment. The American Civilization master's program, from its inception in 1966, listed restoration of architecture and interior design as one of its subject areas; this appears to have been the first effort to turn it into curriculum.

In the fall of 1973, the School of Architecture began to offer the master of architecture in historic preservation. In the context of the school, it was one of several specialty tracks created in the growing master of architecture program (another was Design with Climate, forerunner of today's Sustainable Design program). In a national

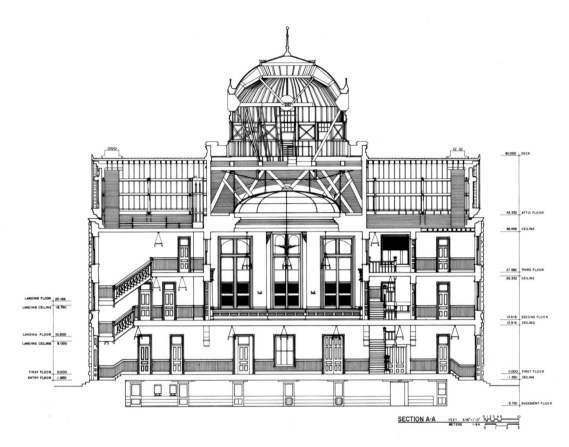

Ryadi Adityavarman (MSAS '96), Colorado County Courthouse: The Winedale Preservation Institute, 1993.
This was part of a set of HABS-standard drawings awarded second place in the national Peterson Prize competition.

context, this was the fifth preservation graduate program in the U.S., and the first west of the Mississippi River.

Bell joined the full-time Architecture faculty in 1975, when Roy Graham left to follow Gene George as Resident Architect at Colonial Williamsburg. That summer, he launched the Winedale Preservation Institute, a four-week immersion experience devoted to measuring and drawing the historic structures of Winedale and the surrounding area and learning the principles and practices of preservation. During the week, students were expected to remain at the Center, and no guests were permitted. "When we had money we had a cook, and when we didn't," recalls Wayne, he and other faculty "came in after a day of fieldwork and did the cooking." The residency boundaries were interpreted to include the general store down the street, where one could drink a cold beer on the porch at the end of a hot day.

The institute enrolled UT students beyond the School of Architecture and, also, students from Texas A&M University, the University of Houston, and other schools.

It was a requirement for students entering UT's Graduate Program in Historic Preservation, for whom it provided a memorable orientation. "It was a place and time of magical proportions, which changed my life," recalled Bess Althaus Graham, Winedale '76.[3] Gerlinde Leiding joined Wayne on the Winedale faculty from the beginning, and, later, so did Dan Leary (both also taught preservation courses back on campus in Austin).

The Architectural Conservation Laboratory dates from the early 1980s. The National Conservation Advisory Council issued a Blue Book of standards for conservation education and facilities. The school's renovation of Goldsmith Hall provided an opportunity to address the standards more rigorously here than at most other universities. Bell consulted with an outside expert from Columbia University, Fran Gale, for advice on setting up a state-of-the-art facility. The lab opened in a purpose-designed space in the basement of the Goldsmith addition. Conservation became, and has remained, a distinctive strength of UT's program.

The master of science in architectural studies (MSAS) degree, beginning in 1983, broadened the horizon for the preservation program. The master of architecture in historic preservation could produce only preservation architects—it was an accredited architecture degree— at a time when professional roles in the field were increasingly diverse. The MSAS enabled historians, planners, and conservators (as well as other designers such as landscape architects and interior designers) to gain professional education in preservation alongside architects. To better align our degree with emerging standards in the field, its name was changed to the MS in Historic Preservation in 2003, which graduated its first class in 2004.

Wayne Bell retired from the UT faculty in 1995. Jeffrey Chusid, previously director of the Historic Preservation program at the University of Southern California, came to direct our program from 1998 to 2005. Chusid brought new emphases on international preservation practice and cultural landscapes. Over the past few years, through the interests of faculty and students, the program has developed a focus on modernism and the recent past. Under Dean Larry Speck, an expanded Conservation Laboratory moved to the new Materials Resource Center in West Mall Building in Fall 2002, funded by the University Co-op.

We came in the 2006-2007 academic year—Michael from the University of Colorado, where he founded the Graduate Program in Historic Preservation and the Colorado Center for Preservation Research, and Fran from Prosoco, an industry leader in masonry conservation, and, before that, the National Center for Preservation Technology and Training. Fran is the first full-time Conservation Lab director and conservation faculty member. Both of us reinforce the school's strength in preservation research, which dates back all the way to Sam Gideon.

Historic preservation is a track in each of the school's PhD programs in Architecture and Community and Regional Planning. The program enrolled its first PhD student in 1999.

Funded research in the past four years includes over $400,000 in federal, state, city, and foundation grants. Projects range from conservation science (for the National Park Service, investigating how to stabilize historic burial grounds at Cape Lookout National Seashore) to web-based media (an online wiki tool to explore social collaboration in community historical surveys). A 2007 grant from the Getty Foundation allowed faculty and students to develop a preservation plan for UT's historic Forty Acres. Our recommendations for maintaining historic buildings and landscapes will become part of the Campus Sustainability Policy.

In the school's centennial year, we are strengthening the program's connection to design with a new preservation track in the MArch II post-professional degree and through faculty shared with Interior Design. With support from the Meadows Foundation, we are integrating sustainability into the preservation curriculum. We continue the long tradition of working with the other programs in the school and other units across the campus to provide opportunities for coursework and research in allied disciplines. We have come to know and treasure alumni from the program's almost four decades, who are distributed around the world and around the many quarters of the profession. Our students are well prepared to join them as the field's leaders.

[1] U.S. Conference of Mayors, *With Heritage So Rich* (1966; 2d ed., Washington, D. C.: Preservation Press, 1983). The same year, Drury Blakeley Alexander published the landmark *Texas Homes of the Nineteenth Century* (Austin: University of Texas Press, 1966).

[2] Gaynell Doehne, "Architecture Has a New Mission," *Alcalde* (July 1972), 10.

[3] "A Reunion for Participants, Faculty, Lecturers, Staff & Friends of the Winedale Institute in Historic Preservation," Nov. 6, 1993.

Expanding the Field: Origins of the Landscape Architecture Program

Hope Hasbrouck, Assistant Professor. Faculty member since 2004.
Jason Sowell, Assistant Professor. Faculty member since 2005.
Allan W. Shearer, Assistant Professor. Faculty member since 2009.

ENTERING INTO ONLY ITS eighth year and graduating only four classes, the Graduate Program in Landscape Architecture has made significant strides in preparing the next generation of design professionals and in advancing professional discourse. It has been listed as high as eleventh in annual rankings of national landscape architecture programs by *Design Intelligence* report, and in 2009, it was named as one of three internationally notable landscape architecture programs by *Azure* magazine of Canada. Its students have received prestigious internships with firms such as Design Workshop, SWA Group, and Peter Walker and Partners; and they have earned six Texas Chapter American Society of Landscape Architecture Merit Awards and one national Honor Award. The faculty has garnered several academic fellowships and teaching accolades.

These achievements rest firmly on the early work of forceful faculty, practitioners, and administrators from across the school, the university, the state, and the nation. This group of dedicated individuals stood behind the school's belief that landscape architecture was an essential part of its agenda to undertake research and educate students to develop a sustainable world.

The appointment of Fritz Steiner as dean was viewed by the school's faculty as an important step for advancing its green agenda and for the expansion of interdisciplinary bridges. An essential component of

Simon Atkinson and the first landscape architecture studio in London, 2003

advanced architecture students designed two memorials along Austin's Shoal Creek. Additionally, Olin presented a lecture series in which he positioned the practice of landscape architecture within scholarly debates and sustainable agendas. The studio's work and his lectures were published in the book, *Landscape: Memory. Expression. Representation.*[1] Beyond his administrative role, Dean Steiner also contributed to the intellectual foundation for landscape architectural studies by offering his course Environmental Readings, which examines the texts that underlie ecological design practices.

During its inaugural academic year of 2003–2004, attention was given to introducing professionals and academics to the new program and to developing its curriculum. In the fall semester, Dean Steiner and Professor Atkinson, now the first director of the Landscape Architecture program, brought together an energetic and accomplished faculty. Austin designer Jill Nokes and Gary Smith, RLA, with Professor Robin Abrams from Texas A&M University, taught alongside Dean Steiner and the principals Todd Johnson and Kurt Culbertson from Design Workshop in Colorado. Atkinson, drawing on funds from the Mike Hogg Centennial Professorship in Community and Regional Planning, which he holds, took the entering students to London for their introductory studio. This beginning at the heart of a great city set the trajectory for the program's pedagogical development and established the strong intellectual links between the school's Urban Design and Landscape Architecture programs, which continue today.

this vision was a graduate-level landscape architecture program. Beginning in 2001, long-time faculty member Simon Atkinson worked alongside Dean Steiner to develop a formal proposal and marshal it through the university's internal approval process. The strong support of Provost Sheldon Ekland-Olson and Graduate School Dean Teresa Sullivan added momentum to the effort as committees within the school established the curriculum and sought instructors. Then in December of 2002, Dr. Sullivan, who had become Executive Vice Chancellor of the University of Texas System, received the news that the Texas Higher Education Coordinating Board had granted approval of the master of landscape architecture degree program and the school's ability to award first- and post-professional master's degrees.

With approval in hand, the school prepared to launch the new program. During the spring of 2002, renowned landscape architect and educator Laurie Olin held the Ruth Carter Stevenson Regents Chair in the Art of Architecture. His role was multivalent. In a studio taught in conjunction with his protégé, Gary R. Smith,

Also in the fall of 2003, two events in the school solidified the presence and scholastic position of landscape architecture as mediator between cultural practices and ecological forces and introduced the program to the national scholastic discourse. The first was a workshop on Civic Environmentalism organized, in part, by Steven Moore, director of the Sustainable Design program. The second was the Landscape Architecture Foundation's Futures Initiative symposium, Connectivity and Landscape Change, organized by Anne Beamish and Barbara Parmenter, of the Community and Regional Planning program. As noted participants, such as Anne Whiston Spirn, the late Bill Mitchell, Darrel Morrison, Grant Jones, Julie Bargmann, and Steward Pickett spoke of landscape's future, the MLA students and faculty positioned their own.

Further advancement came the following year when, in the fall of 2004, Professor Emeritus E. Lynn Miller, from Penn State University arrived to initiate the program's process toward accreditation. With his guidance, the program achieved candidacy status from the Landscape Architecture Accreditation Board (LAAB) in 2005. In the fall of 2005, Professor Dean Almy became director of the program, intensifying its focus on the urban landscape. After graduating its first class of professional students in the spring of 2006, the program stood for LAAB accreditation in the fall. Full accreditation was awarded in January of 2007.

Since the inception of the program, the faculty has used curricular strength and quality instruction as the means to develop an accomplished student body and strong institutional reputation. Central to this plan is a rigorous and coordinated four-semester core curriculum followed by two semesters of flexible advanced studio and elective courses. The program's intellectual and pedagogical development followed from the addition of a diverse group of tenured or tenure-track teachers, each of whom paired strong design backgrounds with expertise in the program's curricular areas. The three design studio instructors Hope Hasbrouck (MArch, MLA, FAAR), Allan Shearer (MLA, PhD), and Jason Sowell (BArch, MLA) developed courses in visual communication, planning theory and methods, and technology, respectively; in turn, each contributed to the core studios' emphasis on inquiry, aesthetics, scale, and appropriate detail resolution. In like manner, Miroslava Beneš (PhD, FAAR) developed the program's history and theory course sequence; Sarah Dooling (PhD) established the natural systems course sequence; and Dean Almy (BArch, MArch UD) created courses and studios that focused on contemporary urban theory and questions of infrastructure and density.

Beyond the school, the Landscape Architecture program has developed teaching and research alliances across the university. Of particular importance to the program's course offerings and research agenda were ties forged with the Department of Geography, the College of Natural Sciences, and the Lady Bird Johnson Wildflower Center. The Wildflower Center, an organized research unit administered by the school and the College of Natural Sciences, led the Sustainable Sites Initiative (SSI) in conjunction with the ASLA and the U.S. Botanic Garden; the SSI set forth guidelines and performance measures in the design, construction, and maintenance of sites.

In looking forward to the future of landscape architecture within the school, it is fitting to recall the original aims of the discipline. In 1914, just five years after the ASLA was created and four years after the founding of the School of Architecture, Charles W. Eliot introduced landscape architecture to the readers of *National Geographic* by writing that it would become, "the most direct professional contributor to the improvement of the human environment."[2] It would do so by understanding the interrelated needs of improving towns and cities and of conserving natural resources. As the profession continues to work toward this ambition, we also recognize the observation made by historian and critic J.B. Jackson that the making of landscape is, fundamentally, the speeding up or slowing down of natural processes, and that through this making, a society gives comprehendible form to its environment.[3] As such, practice operates on and within the complex matrix of inseparable relationships between social practices and environmental processes. We suggest that the disciplinary success of landscape architecture will be measured by our ability to act in a manner that gives form to the goals of sustainable health, safety, welfare, and aesthetics of cultures and their environments. And in turn, the Graduate Program in Landscape Architecture will find its success in the conveyance of knowledge and skills to identify, evaluate, and effect positive change to those interrelationships within the built environment.

LANDSCAPE ARCHITECTURE FACULTY 2003-2010

Robin Abrams	Dean Almy	Kira Appelhans	Simon Atkinson	Miroslava Beneš	Ethne Clarke	Kelley Crews-Meyer
Kurt Culbertson	Sarah Dooling	Ilse Frank	Kate Hansen	Hope Hasbrouck	Todd Johnson	Jason Kentner
Laura Knott	Kimberly Kohlhaas	Christopher Lalich	Eleanor McKinney	E. Lynn Miller	Catherine O'Connor	Laurie D. Olin
Lynn Osgood	Joyce Rosner	Mario Schjetnan	Allan Shearer	Keith Shuley	Mark Simmons	W. Gary Smith
Jason Sowell	Thomas Spencer	Frederick Steiner	Richard P. Swallow	Steve Windhager	Nichole Wiedemann	Kenneth Young

[1] W. Gary Smith, ed., *Landscape: Memory. Expression. Representation.* (Austin: School of Architecture, The University of Texas at Austin, 2002).

[2] Charles W. Eliot, "The Need of Conserving the Beauty and Freedom of Nature in Modern Life," *National Geographic* (July 1914), 67-73.

[3] John Brinckerhoff Jackson,"The Word Itself," in *Discovering the Vernacular Landscape* (New Haven: Yale University Press, 1984), 3-8.

Charles Moore and Graduate Studies

In 1984, Charles W. Moore was appointed the O'Neil Ford Centennial Chair of Architecture, the school's first endowed faculty position. The world-renowned architect, then fifty-eight, came to Austin to lead the post-professional graduate program in architecture. Collaboration and travel were hallmarks of Moore's studios. His students investigated a wide range of unconventional topics, including vernacular and popular building practices, and worked with him on large-scale design problems and exhibitions. Among these projects were studies for a world's fair in Chicago.

Moore's trace on campus is evident in parts of Goldsmith and Battle Halls and, above all, in the expansion of the Etter-Harbin Alumni Center that he designed with faculty colleague Richard Dodge in 1989.

Moore received the AIA Gold Medal in 1991, two years before his death. Students and staff expressed their pride in his achievement by wearing "Charles is Golden" buttons. The Charles W. Moore Archives, housed in the Alexander Architectural Archive, includes drawings, prints, correspondence, books, and other materials from his prolific career. His home and studio now house the Charles Moore Center for the Study of Place and Colin Rowe's personal architectural library.

Hal Box and Charles Moore, 1984

Left: World's Fair Project; Charles Moore, critic, 1988-89

Below: Moore with his students in Taos, NM, 1987

Ida Polzer
(MArch II '10)
Models for
adaptive re-use
of historic
buildings in
Dubrovnik:
Master's Design
Study, Steven
Moore, critic

GRADUATE STUDIES IN ARCHITECTURE

UT authorized a MS in Architecture in 1912, just three years after launching the BS degree. The oldest theses in the library date from 1930 and include Robert Leon White's (BS '21, MS '30) study of Mission San José y San Miguel de Aguayo in San Antonio. White earned his degree while serving as a faculty member and as the university's Supervising Architect, in which capacity he played a key role in adapting the vocabulary of Spanish colonial architecture to the campus. Like the MS, the MArch, established in 1934, initially was a post-professional degree. Among the oldest MArch theses is "Progressive Architecture for the Negro Baptist Church," by John Saunders Chase (MArch '52), the school's first African American student.

In the 1970s, deans Taniguchi, Burnette, and Box made a concerted effort to encourage faculty research and raise the profile of graduate education. Richard Swallow, serving as graduate advisor, increased enrollment in the MArch program by broadening its scope to include first-professional students and tracks in historic preservation and sustainable design. The school restructured the MS in Architectural Studies in 1983 to open the specialized programs to students without professional degrees in architecture. In recent years the school has renamed the degree to better represent the programs' disciplinary identities (MS Historic Preservation, MS Urban Design, MS Sustainable Design, MA Architectural History, MSAS Interdisciplinary Studies). A PhD program in architectural history and historic preservation was established in 1994, and the Graduate School's interdisciplinary PhD option has become a vehicle for students seeking advanced study in sustainable design.

In 2010, the graduate programs in Architecture – professional, post-professional, and academic – accounted for nearly 250 of the 750 students enrolled in the school. Of these, approximately 190 constituted the first- and post-professional MArch programs. The topics of the three theses cited for excellence in 2009-10 suggest the range of research interests: Li Tong (MSHP '10), prototype analysis for high-density building in Austin's historic Warehouse District; Kristi Katherine Marks (MSSD '10), critical study of "black box" methodologies underlying planning of a renewable energy grid in Algeria; and Ida Polzer (post-professional MArch '10), investigation of cultural and environmental sustainability in Dubrovnik, Croatia.

Some Observations on the Last Twenty-Five Years at the School of Architecture

Anthony Alofsin, Roland Gommel Roessner Centennial Professor in Architecture. Faculty member since 1987.

THREE DEVELOPMENTS strike me as particularly significant during the last quarter century in the history of the School of Architecture. The first is the expansion of the scope of graduate study in architecture. In 1987, the enrollment of the graduate students was relatively small, but over the next decades, the numbers of enrolled students grew; their general quality increased; and their curriculum expanded in scope and rigor. While the undergraduate program retained its traditional strengths and reputation, graduate training in architecture caught up, so that by the time of the school's centennial, both programs had accelerated in national rankings of architecture schools to be among the best in the country.

The second factor of significance is the founding of the PhD program in architecture, which allowed an advancement in the school's intellectual agenda. Dean Hal Box provided the impetus for creating the program. He believed that the future of the school lay in the pursuit of advanced research and charged me, the first instructor with a doctoral degree in architectural history, with creating a program and leading it through the required approvals. The late Francisco Arumí-Noe, a specialist in solar design, participated, and while the charter of the PhD program was broadly based, it originally emphasized architectural history which was, with its doctoral faculty and range of courses, the only field that provided adequate depth for doctoral work.

The process of getting the various approvals within the school, the university, and the state took over six years. The resulting program was rigorous in its requirements and required a master's degree for entry. As the expertise of the faculty broadened with new appointments of teachers with advanced training, the PhD program's scope extended. At the same time the parallel doctoral program in planning surged in terms of the numbers of students enrolled. Under Dean Fritz Steiner, who succeeded Dean Larry Speck, the school's direction has shifted toward environmental issues, sustainability, and planning, and advanced research has flourished in those fields. Dean Box's dream has taken form and expanded with the school's move into a growth area in design education.

The third development of significance focuses on the founding of the Center for American Architecture and Design. The Center resulted from the support of Dean Box and the efforts of Blake Alexander and Larry Speck, who were co-directors from 1982 to 1984. Building upon Speck's directorship (1984-1990), which saw the broadening and solidification of its programs, I served as director from 1990 to 1993. A support group, Friends of the Center, was created (and later merged into the Friends of Architecture), and the Center's reputation widened nationally and internationally. Not only did the frequent symposia draw an increased focus on the school, but the annual publications of the award-winning *CENTER* journal provided a national forum for ideas. Reflecting a wide range of scholarly and academic expertise as well as thematic variety, they remain in print. Michael Benedikt has assumed the directorship, emphasizing a well attended Friday in-house lecture series and providing a new series of publications and symposia, many of them international in scope.

In sum, these developments have helped the school move from being known as an institution providing architectural practitioners with highly proficient and reliable workers to an intellectual environment that prizes critical thinking as well as the accumulation of skills of the trade.

The Next Hundred Years

Eric Hepburn, Director of Information Technology since 2003.

*Improving lives through the responsible
design of enduring places and communities.*

-Core Purpose of the School of Architecture

This year the School of Architecture turns 100 years old.
From some points of view, one hundred years is a long
time. It is 52,560,000 minutes and 36,500 sunrises. It
is the length of four American familial generations, and
it is five times older than the Internet.

One hundred years of age is on the scale of many things
that we take for granted. Air conditioning, electrical
power distribution, and coal-fired power plants are all
about 108 years old. Gasoline combustion engines and
steam turbines, which generate about 80 percent of

global electric power, are about 125. The electric motor
turns 189 this year and the dominant use of fossil fuels
for energy turns 210.

On other scales, one hundred is a blip. Written language
is about 6,000 years old, while human civilizations are
about 14,000. Our species is about 195,000 years old,
while animals, in general, developed about 580,000,000
years ago. Multi-cellular life is about 1,000,000,000
years old, and single-celled organisms date back about
3,000,000,000 years. Our planet is about 4,450,000,000
years old, and our universe is about 13,750,000,000.

These comparisons help contextualize the variety of temporal scales with which the disciplines of architecture and planning must deal. The last hundred years of the School of Architecture, and for that matter of Western civilization, have been spent focusing on the short and the medium term, while ignoring the long-term scale. By invoking the core purpose of the school, I will suggest ways to incorporate the long-term scale into our thinking and our processes, so that, in our next one hundred years, we can realize the school's aspiration of producing enduring places and communities.

The Energy Bubble and Modernity

The largest contributor to our current temporal myopia is the energy bubble. The discovery and harnessing of the vast amounts of energy stored in fossil fuels has produced a world full of abundant and available energy that has fundamentally restructured our perspective on our relationship with the universe. This abundant energy combined with Enlightenment ideas about the freedom of human intellect and its capacity to escape the fetters of our animal nature has produced a human culture that believes itself to be materially and spiritually superior to and disconnected from earthly ecologies. We have believed that we and our creations are limited only by our own imaginations, and we have been wrong.

The energy bubble was produced by an illusion, the belief that fossil fuel energy is cheap and that it costs whatever amount of human labor and technology was required to extract it from the ground and process it. What we are discovering about fossil fuels and a great many modern practices is that there are many externalities, the costs of remediating or mitigating the damage caused by our practices. The true cost of a gallon of gas is not only in the oil well, the transport, the processing, and the delivery; it is also in contamination cleanup, carbon sequestration, health care costs, and biosphere restoration. Ignorance about these externalities does not mitigate their impacts.

Our modern misconceptions about ourselves have amplified these problems. We have subscribed to the Enlightenment idea of our own superior rationality even in the face of decades of research from psychology and economics that demonstrates that we are not rational beings. The rational processes that are part of our verbal cognitive experience of consciousness are a very small part of the total human system. This is why it is easy to make resolutions and hard to keep them. It is why it is so easy to rationalize our own actions, while demonizing the actions of others.

We cling to the illusions of cheap energy and rational selves at our own peril. Ninety-seven percent of all the species that have lived on this earth are now extinct. The one thing working to our advantage is that we are the first species to realize this.

Improving Lives

The first thing that we have to realize about improving lives is that our rejection of the fallacy of rational superiority is also a rejection of disconnectedness, from each other and other forms of life. Humans are an ultra-social species; our survival is dependent on our collective behaviors, structures, and institutions. Similarly, we cannot improve, support, or sustain our own lives without taking into consideration all of the lifeforms in the biosphere of which we are a part, and, as projects like Biosphere 2 demonstrate, our comprehension of ecologies is still in its infancy.

In order to improve lives, the School of Architecture must be contextual in its approach and vigilant and comprehensive in its integration of human and biological ecologies. This approach must be grounded in regional understandings of place and must include global considerations of impact.

This contextual understanding must also embrace and account for the nature of humanity itself. This will require the ability to close the loop between the discoveries of psychologists, sociologists, and economists, and the practice of architects and planners. The next century will demand that our practitioners are more broadly educated and more solidly grounded.

Responsible Design

Design must be responsible to the needs, but not the whims, of individuals, societies, and ecologies. Our responsibilities must be determined by data-driven and theory-producing inquiries into the truth of our current situation. These responsibilities must then be operationalized into metrics, which we can model and measure. This is the key role of information technology in the next century. The computer and Internet have enabled us to radically re-scale the externalization, sharing, and processing of an exponentially expanding body of information. This emerging capacity for processing promises further radical transformations.

In order to apply these capacities to our core responsibilities, we will need to apply our best ecological, sociological, and psychological theories to produce predictive models that inform these aspects of our designs. I envision these tools as micro-applications that involve iterative processes of "human-hand" with real-time simulation feedback. For instance, an energy analysis micro-application that generates rough insolation and heat gain/loss calculations based on early massing concepts, regional weather, and local site conditions. This would allow designers to include these factors in the balancing act that is good design. Various stages of design might have micro-applications that plug into form-based building information models such that the designer has an instrument dashboard reporting the analysis of various aspects of the modeled building performance that are relevant to the stage of design. These types of tools would allow the human brain to do what it does best: deal with qualitative aspects of design from a uniquely human perspective, while using computer processing for what it does best: iterative mathematical analysis of logic-based formulations to assess goodness-of-fit, efficiency, and other rational-logical constructs.

Enduring Places and Communities

How can we speak of the meaning of enduring without facing head-on the question of human mortality? To leave something behind, a mark, a monument, a memory... these are some of the primary coping mechanisms that we have developed to confront our fear of death. This fear of death seems to be one of the most significant drawbacks to the system of verbal cognitive consciousness that our species has developed.

Is it enough for our children to endure, or their children, or their children's children? Or do we want this same perpetuation for them and their progeny? At what time scale are we comfortable with the extinction of our own species? Is this aversion simply an extension of our own fear of mortality? Or is it a calling to something greater? Are we capable, as a species, of escaping this planet-bound cycle of extinction?

What is an appropriate aspiration for a school of architecture? Al-Azhar University in Cairo has been in continuous operation for 1,022 years, so, perhaps, 10,000 years would be a more noble goal, or 100,000, or 1,000,000? What would we have to do today to set our sites on 1,000,000 years of architecture and planning? During that million years we can expect shifts in climate and sea level, motion in the Earth's crust, and changes in the biosphere including significant extinction events.

The University of Texas at Austin proudly proclaims: *What starts here changes the world.* The School of Architecture adds that our purpose is *improving lives through the responsible design of enduring places and communities.* In order to fulfill these claims, in order not to be just another species that came and went, changed by the world, we will have to tackle our own biggest problem of scale, the temporal one. In order to do this, we will need to apply all of the amazing technology that we have developed in combination with all of the knowledge and wisdom that we possess to close the loop between what we understand and how we live. Architecture and planning have an enormous role to play in this transformation. It is time to get started on the next one hundred years.

A Century of Student Work

This portfolio presents student work from each of the ten decades that span the school's history from its founding in 1910 to 2010. Most of the images have been drawn from the holdings of the Alexander Architectural Archive, which continues to collect student work in the form of drawings, photographs, and, increasingly, digital files. The collection depends on the generosity of alumni willing to share their student work and, consequently, is neither comprehensive nor systematic in scope. Nevertheless, it traces many of the themes that have guided design education in the School of Architecture over the past one hundred years.

Work from the Centennial Alumni Exhibition

Students eventually become alumni and enter the world of professional practice. The school invited Stephen Sharpe, the editor of *Texas Architect*, to make selections from the rich body work offered by alumni for exhibition in the Mebane Gallery in November 2010.

Thomas D. Broad (BS '15), 9-Hour Sketch Problem; A Restaurant and Observatory on the Top of a Mountain: Senior Year, Architectural Design, 1915

Roger Q. Small, A Country Club: Architectural Design, 1915/1916

Roger Q. Small, Tower Project: Architectural Design, 1915/1916

Thomas D. Broad (BS '15), Charcoal Drawing: Sophomore Year, 1913

Alma Jacobs (BArch '17), Charcoal Drawing: Sophomore Year, 1915

Norman Max Arlitt, Watercolor Study: Summer Session, 1915

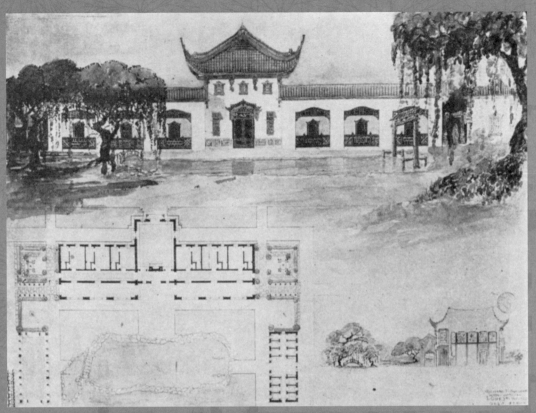

Richard A. Bouchard, A Guest House: Junior Year Design, 1927/1928

Roy White (BS '29), A Guest House: Junior Year Design, 1928

Lewis M. Hamby (BArch '29), An Observatory: Senior Year Design, 1928

"A MISSION IN CENTRAL CHINA" · JACK W. EVANS

Jack W. Evans (BArch '38), A Mission in Central China, 1938

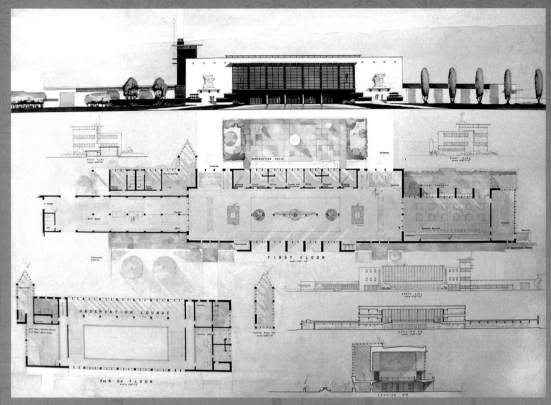

Joseph W. Baxter (BArch '39), A Municipal Air Terminal for Austin, Texas: Fifth Year Thesis Problem, 1939

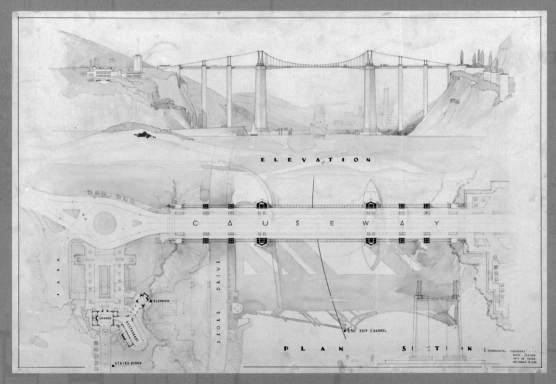

Wolf Jessen (BArch '36), A Monumental Causeway, 1935

Student Work 1940s

William G. Wagner (BArch '49), A Glider Pilots' Club, 1946

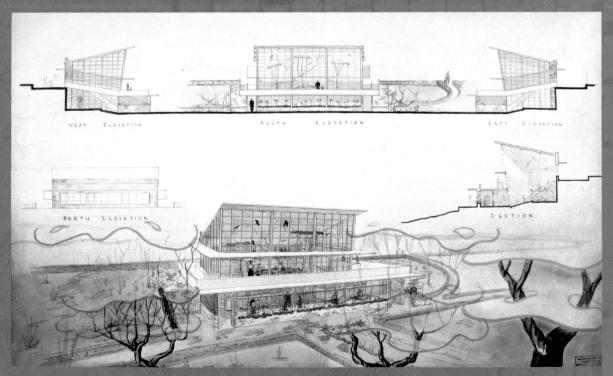

Joseph Russell Coleman, A Zoological Garden and Aviary, 1946

Peyton Edward Kirven (BArch '48), A Casino on an Island, 1947

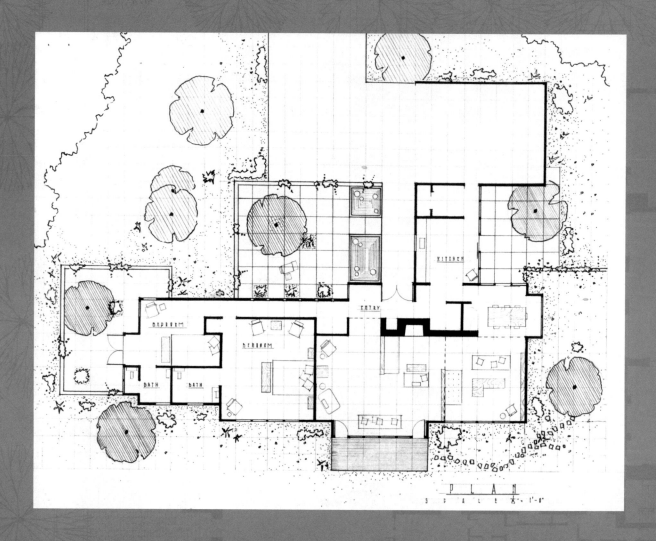

Raymond Studer (BArch '57), Interpretation of a Plan, plan and perspective: Junior
Year, John Hejduk and Bernhard Hoesli, critics, 1955

Thomas Vernon Trainer (BArch '57), Interpretation of a Plan, perspective: Junior Year, John Hejduk and Bernhard Hoesli, critics, 1955

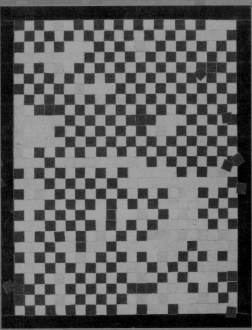

W. Bryan Thruston (BArch '57), Composition: Junior Year, Robert Slutzky, Irving Rubin, and Lee Hirsche, critics, 1955

Albert K. H. Tung (BArch '57), An Interrupted Pattern Study: Junior Year, Robert Slutzky, Irving Rubin, and Lee Hirsche, critics, 1955

Bimmer, residence project, 1968

"A Flexible Habitable Space," constructed on the West Mall, 1969

Marshall Wilson (BArch '69), Train Station for Georgetown, Texas: Fourth Year Project, ca. 1968

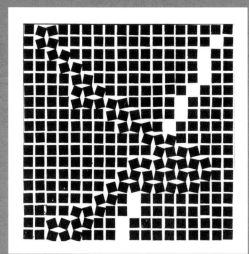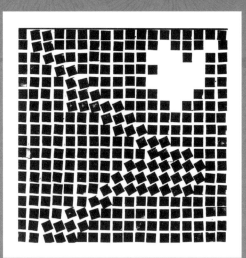

Pam Zeigler, Modular Constellations: First Year Design, 1968/1969

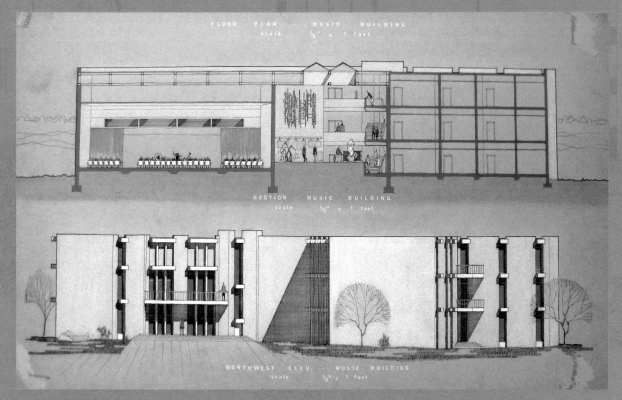

Elmer T. Hodges, Jr. (BArch '65), Music Building: Fifth Year Thesis Project, 1965.

Frank Dunckel (BArch '78), untitled project, 1975

Charles L. Leonard (BArch '75), shade and shadow building study: Jorge Divino, critic, 1973

Robert J. Reid (BArch '75), mixed-use high rise with lobby detail: Jon Bowman, critic, 1975

Bridge project, model: Richard Swallow, critic, 1989

Mimi Garza-Love (BArch '89), Broadway State Office Building: Natalie de Blois, critic, 1989

Robert W. Harding (MArch '88), Aerobic Health and Fitness Center, 1988 TSA Student Design Competition: Gerlinde Leiding, critic, 1988

Jamie Lofgren (MArch '87), Museum of the American Indian, TSA Student Design Competition: Charles Moore, critic, 1986

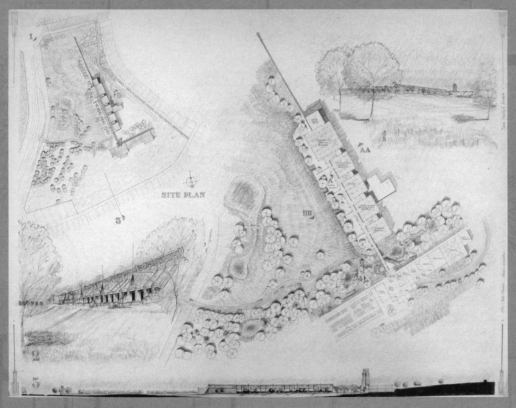

David R. Maxwell (MArch '87), Museum of the American Indian, TSA Student Design Competition: Charles Moore, critic, 1986

WALL SECTION
SCALE 1/4" = 1' - 0"

DETAIL ELEVATION - TYPICAL WALL
SCALE 1/4" = 1' - 0"

James R. Ehler (BArch '94), new student health center, elevation and axonometric: Sinclair Black, critic, 1994

B. Harris, child's chair: Mike Farmer, critic, 1991

Student work exhibit, Mebane Gallery, May 1994

Danelle Briscoe (BArch '95), Baker Center: Fifth Year Studio, Elizabeth Danze, critic, 1995

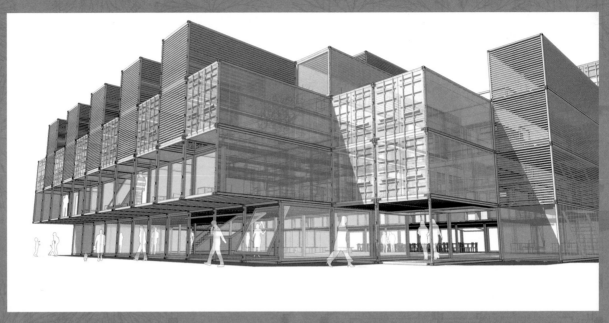

Andrew Torres (MArch '07), School of Architecture Building in São Paulo: Advanced Studio, Barbara Hoidn, critic, 2007

Yan Yau (MLA '10), Republic Square: Graduate
Landscape Studio, Jason Sowell, critic, 2009

Garrett Seaman (BSID '07), Fluor Corporation Headquarters:
Advanced Interior Design Studio, Carl Matthews, critic, 2008

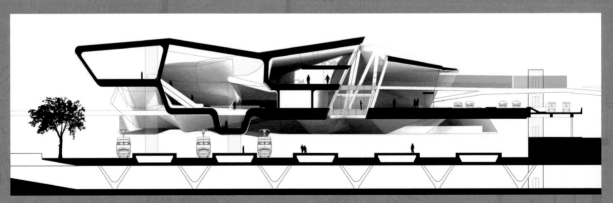

Bhujon Kang, Austin Central Station: Advanced Studio, Werner Lang and Wilfried Wang, critics, 2009

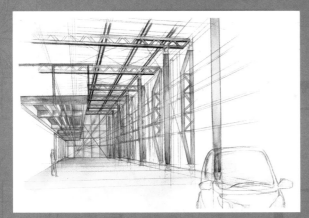

Emily Teng (BArch '10), Smart Car Dealership:
Third Year Sound Building Studio, Ulrich Dangel, critic, 2008

Melissa Eckerman (MArch '09), Pottery Museum and Studio:
Graduate Vertical Studio, Christine Mueller, critic, 2006

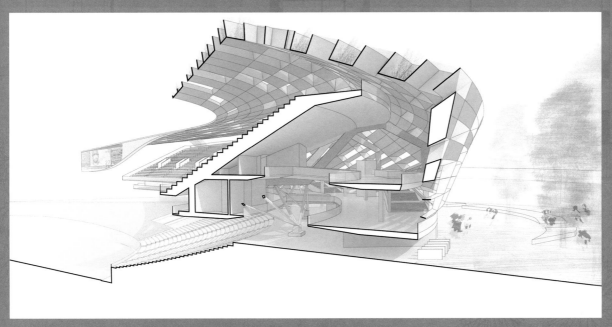

Kevin Johnson (MArch '10), Boston Fan Pier Redevelopment Baseball Stadium Project:
Advanced Studio, Michael Beaman, critic, 2010

RICK ARCHER (BARCH '79)

Lady Bird Johnson Wildflower Center,
Austin, TX, 1995
Overland Partners

SINCLAIR BLACK (BARCH '62)

Great Streets Master Plan, Austin, TX, 2000
Black + Vernooy

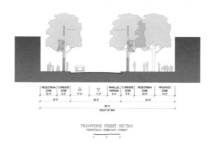

MARLA BOMMARITO-CROUCH (BSID '76)

Lance Armstrong Foundation, Austin, TX, 2009
The Bommarito Group

HANS BUTZER (BARCH '90)

Skydance Bridge, Oklahoma City, OK, 2008
Butzer Design Partnership and
MKEC Engineering

BRIAN CARLSON (BARCH '98)

Robbs Run Residence, Austin, TX, 2005
McKinney York Architects

GARY CUNNINGHAM (BARCH '76)

Cistercian Abbey Church, Irving, TX, 1992
Cunningham Architects

JAMES DODSON (BARCH '95)

Arts Alliance Mobile Performance Venue,
project
Various Architects

CRAIG DYKERS (BARCH '85) AND ELAINE MOLINAR (BARCH '88)

The Norwegian National Opera and Ballet,
Oslo, Norway, 2008
Snøhetta

Alumni Exhibition

JOHN FRANE (BARCH '93)

Center of Gravity Foundation Hall,
Jemez Springs, NM, 2003
Predock_Frane Architects

JORGE GONZALEZ (BARCH '90)

One Arts Plaza,
Dallas, TX, 2007
Morrison Seifert Murphy and Corgan Associates Inc.

KARLA GREER (BARCH '79)

Bartlit Residence,
Castle Pines, CO
Lake | Flato Architects

HOZEFA HAIDERY (MARCH '03)

The Bridge: Homeless Assistance Center,
Dallas, TX, 2008
Overland Partners

ROBERT HARRIS (MARCH '92)

World Birding Center, Mission, TX, 2004
Lake | Flato Architects

PAUL HAYDU (MARCH '95) AND HULETT JONES (BARCH '93)

Coffee Bar, San Francisco, CA, 2008
Jones | Haydu

JULIE HOWARD (BARCH '91)

Malot-Painlévé-la Bruyère School Complex,
Lille, France, 2008
Vong Design Collaborative

BRIAN KORTE (MARCH '94)

Armstrong Oil & Gas, Denver, CO, 2008
Lake | Flato Architects

DAVID LAKE (BSAS '77)

*UT Health Science Center at Houston School of Nursing
and Student Community Center, Houston, TX, 2004
Lake | Flato Architects*

BILLY LAWRENCE (BARCH '78)

*Adoption Facility, Humane Society of San Antonio
and Bexar County, 2002
Alamo Architects*

GREG PAPAY (MARCH '93)

*Francis Parker School, San Diego, CA, 2009
Lake | Flato Architects*

ANAND PARTHASARATHY (MSSD '07) AND KANCHANA SEKAR

Kanchanam Residence, Sivakasi, India, 2009

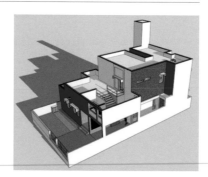

ROBERT SHEMWELL (MARCH '86)

Texas A&M University Bonfire Memorial,
College Station, TX, 2004
Overland Partners

GARY SKOTNICKI (BARCH '74)

Hill County Courthouse Restoration,
Hillsboro, TX, 1993-1999
ARCHITEXAS

TRACY STONE (MARCH '85)

Los Angeles North Central Animal Services Center,
Los Angeles, CA, 2007
Tracy A. Stone Architect

TOM TORNBJERG (MARCH '05)

The Peninsula Residence, Austin, Texas, 2008
Bercy Chen Studio, LP

JAMES VIRA (BARCH '95)

Rapidly Deployable Inflatable Containers, 2008
Viraline

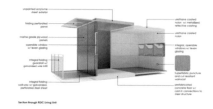

CYNTHIA WALSTON (BARCH '82)

Texas Children's Hospital Feigin Center,
Houston, TX, 2009
FKP Architects

AMIR YAZDAN (BARCH '80)

Shahrzad Commercial and Office Building Complex,
project

MEHRDAD YAZDANI (BArch '84)

UC San Diego Price Center East, San Diego, CA, 1989
Yazdani Studio of Cannon Design

Faculty and Staff, Fall Semester 2010

PROFESSOR

Anthony Alofsin
Kevin Alter
Simon Atkinson
Michael Benedikt
J. Sinclair Black
Richard Cleary

Michael Garrison
David Heymann
Terry Kahn
Nancy Kwallek
Christopher Long
Juan Miró

Steven Moore
Lawrence Speck
Frederick Steiner
Wilfried Wang
Patricia Wilson

ASSOCIATE PROFESSOR

Dean Almy
Miroslava Beneš
Kent Butler
Elizabeth Danze
Larry Doll
Louise Harpman

Michael Holleran
Werner Lang
Carl Matthews
Smilja Milovanovic-Bertram
Michael Oden
Robert Paterson

Vincent Snyder
Danilo Udovicki-Selb
Lois Weinthal
Nichole Wiedemann
Ming Zhang

ASSISTANT PROFESSOR

Michael Beaman
Danelle Briscoe
Ulrich Dangel
Sarah Dooling
Matt Fajkus
Tamie Glass

Francisco Gomes
Hope Hasbrouck
Fernando Lara
Ming-Chun Lee
Talia McCray
Elizabeth Mueller

Allan Shearer
Igor Siddiqui
Bjørn Sletto
Jason Sowell

ADJUNCT AND VISITING FACULTY

Elizabeth Alford
Judith Birdsong
John Blood
Coleman Coker
Ernesto Cragnolino
Kimberley Furlong
Fran Gale
Allison Gaskins
Barbara Hoidn
Alan Knox
Christopher Lalich
François Levy

Charlton Lewis
Mark Macek
Deborah Mann
Mark Oberholzer
Clay Odom
Catherine O'Connor
Monica Penick
Rachael Rawlins
Joyce Rosner
Stephen Ross
Jack Sanders
Eva Schone

Clay Shortall
Keith Shuley
Mark Simmons
Gregory Smith
Marla Smith
William Storrer
Charles Thompson
Dason Whitsett
Barbara Wilson
Steven Windhager

EMERITUS FACULTY

D. Blake Alexander
Wayne Bell
Jon Bowman
Hal Box

Owen Cappleman
Peter Coltman
R. James Coote
Daniel Leary

Gerlinde Leiding
Richard Swallow
Lance Tatum
Roxanne Williamson

STAFF

Anita Ahmadi
Scholarship/Fellowship Coordinator

Stuart Bone
*Course Scheduler/Assistant to the Associate
Dean for Graduate Programs*

Elizabeth Cobbe
*Assistant to the Director, Center for American
Architecture and Design*

Jeanne Crawford
Assistant Dean for Undergraduate Programs

Amy Crossette
Director, Public Affairs

Alison Diehl
Office Manager, Office of Information Technology

Jeff Evelyn
Assistant Dean for Administration

Mike Farmer
Facilities Maintenance Manager

Bobby Gonzalez
Travel Coordinator

Rosemin Gopaul
Program Coordinator for Graduate Affairs

Eric Hepburn
Director, Information Technology

Julie Hooper
*Assistant Dean for Development and External
Relations*

Garrett Loontjer
Undergraduate Academic Advisor

Alley Lyles
Events Coordinator

Stacy Manning
*Associate Director for Constituent Relations and
Alumni Affairs*

Christine Marcin
Assistant to the Dean

Maia McCoy
Human Resources Coordinator

Chaz Nailor
Graduate Admissions Coordinator

Carrie O'Malley
Director, Career Services

Judy Parker
Receptionist

Pamela Peters
Publications Editor

Christopher Rankin
Webmaster

Amelia Rey-Shannon
Development Associate

Xavier Sandoval
Accounts Manager/Financial Analyst

Elizabeth Schaub
Director, Visual Resources Collection

Rob Stepnoski
Systems Administrator

Ray Vargas
Procurement Officer

John Vehko
Technical Associate, Design Workshop Lab

Barbara Wilson
*Interim Director, Center for
Sustainable Development*

Christine Wong
*Production Editor, Center for American
Architecture and Design*

AFFILIATED STAFF, ARCHITECTURE AND PLANNING LIBRARY

Donna Coates
*Archives Assistant for Access and Collections
Management*

Beth Dodd
*Head Librarian; Curator,
Alexander Architectural Archives*

Martha González Palacios
Architecture and Planning Librarian

Daniel Orozco
Circulation Services Supervisor

Holly Ovale
Serials Clerk and Night Supervisor

Joseph Sosa
Bibliographic Assistant

Nancy Sparrow
Curatorial Assistant for Public Services

Illustration Credits

Cover: CAH, DI 06017.

Page 4: Top: AAA, University of Texas Buildings Collection, Drawings and Manuscript Material, 1882-ongoing, University of Texas Campuses throughout Texas (UT Buildings Collection); Bottom: Cactus Yearbook 1913, pg 193.

Page 5: Flash Photography, Dallas, TX, 2010.

Page 7: Top: *Cactus Yearbook*, 1912, pg 21; Middle: *Cactus Yearbook*, 1916, pg 30; Bottom: CAH, Goldwin Goldsmith, PPC, DI 06439.

Pages 8-10: *Architectural Year Book*, 1914/1915.

Page 11: Courtesy of Kayla Lyssy.

Page 12: Top: AAA, UT Buildings Collection; Bottom: CAH, UT Buildings, Old Engineering, Prints and Photographs Collection (PPC), DI 06087.

Page 13: Top: AAA, UT Buildings Collection; Bottom Left: *Architectural Year Book*, 1927/1928; Bottom Right: CAH, UT Buildings, B. Hall, PPC, DI 06088.

Page 14: Top: CAH, UT Buildings, Architecture, PPC, DI 06089; Bottom Left: Dana Norman, photographer; Bottom Right (interior): CAH, UT Buildings, Architecture, PPC, DI 06090; Bottom Right (exterior): AAA, UT Buildings Collection.

Page 15: Top: UT Staff Photographer, 1987; Bottom: Mike Farmer, photographer, 2010.

Page 16: Top: Marsha Miller, photographer, 2007; Middle: Elise Wasser, photographer, 2010; Bottom: Frederick Steiner, photographer, 2010.

Page 17: Top and Middle: UTSOA staff, photographer; Bottom: Courtesy of David Heymann, Barbara Hoidn, and Wilfried Wang.

Page 19: Left: Bureau of Economic Geology, The University of Texas at Austin; Right: Texas State Library and Archives Commission (Archive Map Number 0929b). Page 20: AAA, Paul Philippe Cret Collection.

Page 21: Left: UTSOA; Right: David Heymann, photographer.

Page 23: Top and Bottom: Courtesy of Roland G. Roessner, Jr.

Page 24: Courtesy of Elizabeth Danze. Page 25: Courtesy of Evan K. Taniguchi.

Page 26: Top: Courtesy of Evan K. Taniguchi; Bottom: Courtesy of Tommy Cowan.

Page 32: Left: *Cactus Yearbook*, 1955, pg 61; Top Right: Courtesy of William Kelley; Bottom Right: *The Austin American* (February 12, 1954): pg A-13.

Page 33: Top and Bottom Left: AAA, Harwell Hamilton Harris Papers, 1903-1990, California, Texas and North Carolina; Top Right: AAA, University of Texas at Austin, School of Architecture Student Work, Drawings, 1915-current, Selected Design Studies Produced by the Students (UT Student Work Collection); Bottom Right: Photograph by PRRISA, Mexico.

Page 37: Courtesy of Larry Doll.

Page 42: Left: *Cactus Yearbook*, 1968, pg 305; Top Right: *Cactus Yearbook*, 1965, pg 140; Bottom Right: *Cactus Yearbook*, 1964, pg 470.

Page 43: Top Left: AAA, University of Texas at Austin, School of Architecture Archives (SOA Collection); Bottom Left: Charles Horn, photographer, 2010; Right Top, Middle, and Bottom: AAA, SOA Collection.

Page 44: Top: *Cactus Yearbook*, 1971, pg 150.

Page 45: Left: CAH, UT Demonstrations, PPC, DI 06084; Right: CAH, UT Demonstrations, PPC, Right: 06085.

Page 47: AAA, UT Buildings Collection.

Page 48: Left: Elise King, photographer; Right: *The Alcalde Magazine*, December 1933, pg 56.

Page 56: Top: CAH, DI 06083; Middle: *Cactus Yearbook*, 1963, pg 21; Bottom: VRC.

Page 57: Top Left and Right: AAA, UT Student Work Collection; Middle: AAA, Hugh L. McMath Papers; Bottom: AAA, UT Student Work Collection.

Page 58: Top Left: Courtesy of Kate Murphy; Top Right: AAA, UT Student Work Collection; Bottom: AAA, UT Buildings Collection.

Page 59: Top Left: AAA, UT Student Work Collection; Bottom Left: Courtesy of Edna Ledesma; Top Right: Courtesy of Alexis Kurland; Middle Right: Courtesy Kate Murphy; Bottom Right: AAA, UT Student Work Collection.

Page 61: Courtesy of Owen Cappleman.

Page 62: Courtesy of Owen Cappleman.

Page 64: Courtesy of Smilja Milovanovic-Bertram.

Page 67: Left: Courtesy of William Kelley; Right: Nichole Wiedeman, photographer.

Page 68: Nichole Wiedemann, photographer.

Page 70: Courtesy of Phil Zimmerman.

Page 76: Courtesy of Christopher Long.

Page 77: Courtesy of Christopher Long.

Page 79: Kathryn Pierce, photographer.

Page 81: Right: UT Office of Public Affairs; Left: CAH, UT Texas Student Publications, PPC, DI 04081.

Page 82: Top: AAA, UT Buildings Collection; Bottom: *Cactus Yearbook*, 1947, pg 207.

Page 83: Top: Debbe Sharpe, photographer; Bottom Left: *Prospectus*,1989, pg 89; Bottom Right: SOA Staff Photographer, 1990.

Page 85: Left: Courtesy of the Prints and Photographs Collection, MIT Museum, Massachusetts Institute of Technology; Middle: CAH, PPC; Right: Frank Armstrong, photographer, CAH, Office of Public Affairs Records.

Page 86: Courtesy of Nancy Kwallek.

Page 89: Courtesy of Garrett Seaman.

Page 90: Courtesy of Brittany Cooper.

Page 91: Courtesy of Sarah Jean Ellis, Jennifer Lee, and Sarah Wistner.

Page 93: Lois Weinthal, photographer.

Page 95: Top: Courtesy of Smithsonian Archives of American Art, Florence Knoll Bassett Papers, 1932-2000; Bottom: Courtesy of Kimberly Cole.

Page 96: Courtesy of Angela Lauer Crum.

Page 98: Top: *Cactus Yearbook*, 1943, pg 40; Bottom: AAA, Hugo Leipziger-Pearce Manuscript Material, Photographs, (1920-(1955-1978)-1990) Community and Regional Planning (Leipziger-Pearce Collection).

Page 99: AAA, UT Student Work Collection.

Page 100: Top: AAA, UT Student Work Collection; Bottom Left and Right: AAA, Leipziger-Pearce Collection.

Page 101: Top: Elizabeth Mueller, photographer; Bottom: Courtesy of Bjørn Sletto.

Page 102: Top and Middle: Courtesy of Dean Almy; Bottom: VRC.

Page 103: Top: Courtesy of Dean Almy; Bottom: AAA, Leipziger-Pearce Collection.

Pages 111-113: Courtesy of Bjørn Sletto.

Pages 115-116: Courtesy of Ming Zhang.

Page 118: Top: Larry Murphy, photographer, *Cactus Yearbook*, 1985, pg 88; Middle and Bottom: AAA, Walter T. Rolfe (1900-1967) Archival records, drawings and paintings, 1920-1967, Architectural Education; Personal Papers.

Page 119: Top: AAA, Hugh L. McMath Papers; Bottom: Ricardo Fernandez, photographer, 2004, courtesy of Juan Miró.

Page 121: UTSOA.

Page 123: Courtesy of Smilja Milovanovic-Bertram.

Page 125: Courtesy of Michael Garrison.

Page 126: Top: Steven Pumphrey, photographer, *Cactus Yearbook*, 1980, pg 185; Bottom: VRC.

Page 127: Steven Pumphrey, photographer, *Cactus Yearbook*, 1980, pg 185.

Page 128: Jim Tetro, Solar Decathlon, photographer.

Pages 131-132: Courtesy of Werner Lang.

Page 134: Top: *Cactus Yearbook*, 1937, pg 143; Bottom: VRC.

Page 135: AAA, UT Student Work Collection.

Page 138: Robin Abrams, photographer.

Page 140: Top: Debbe Sharpe, photographer, 1984, AAA, SOA Collection; Bottom Left: VRC; Bottom Right: Ernesto Zamarripa, photographer, 1987, AAA, SOA Collection.

Page 141: Courtesy of Ida Polzer.

Page 148: Top: *Architectural Year Book*, 1914/1915; Bottom Left and Right: *Architectural Year Book*, 1915/1916.

Page 149: Top: *Architectural Year Book*, 1914/1915; Bottom: *Architectural Year Book*, 1915/1916.

Pages 150-151: *Architectural Year Book*, 1927/1928.

Pages 152-158: AAA, Student Work Collection.

Page 158: Bottom Left: *Cactus Yearbook*, 1969, pg 96.

Page 159: Top: Image, vol. 5-6, 1969; Bottom: AAA, UT Student Work Collection.

Pages 160-161: AAA, UT Student Work Collection.

Page 162: Top Left: AAA, SOA Collection; Top Right: AAA, Natalie de Blois Working Drawings and Students' Studio Work; Bottom: AAA, UT Student Work Collection.

Page 163: AAA, UT Student Work Collection.

Page 164: VRC. Page 165 Top Left and Right: VRC; Bottom: Courtesy of Danelle Briscoe.

Pages 166-167: Courtesy of respective students.

ABBREVIATIONS:

AAA: Alexander Architectural Archive, University of Texas Libraries, The University of Texas at Austin

CAH: Dolph Briscoe Center for American History, The University of Texas at Austin

VRC: Visual Resources Collection, School of Architecture, The University of Texas at Austin

UTSOA: University of Texas at Austin School of Architecture